D1209768

Fact, Fiction, and Forecast

Third Edition

Fact, Fiction, *and* Forecast

Third Edition

NELSON GOODMAN

THE BOBBS-MERRILL COMPANY, INC.
INDIANAPOLIS · NEW YORK

HOUSTON PUBLIC LIBRARY

78-080843-2

R01158 67441

Copyright 1955 in Great Britain by the University of London

Second Edition © 1965, Third Edition © 1973
by The Bobbs-Merrill Company, Inc.
Printed in the United States of America

First Printing

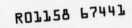

Library of Congress Cataloging in Publication Data
Goodman, Nelson.
Fact, fiction, and forecast.
Includes bibliographical references.
1. Induction (Logic) 2. Conditionals (Logic) 3. Possibility.
4. Forecasting. 5. Science—Philosophy. I. Title.
BC91.G66 1973   161   73-11273
ISBN 0-672-51889-9
ISBN 0-672-61347-6 (pbk.)

CONTENTS

· CONTENTS ·

FOREWORD TO
THE THIRD EDITION

Happily the three rules set forth in the final chapter of the first edition, reduced to two in the second edition, can now be reduced to one. In the second edition, the second of the three rules was dropped since I had found that the cases this rule was designed to cover were taken care of by the first rule. Now, slight modification of the first rule, together with explicit recognition that a hypothesis may at a given time be neither projectible nor unprojectible but rather nonprojectible, has made the third of the original rules also unnecessary. Accordingly IV.4 has been rewritten, and changes thus required in IV.5 have been made.

For this result and others along the way, I am heavily indebted to Robert Schwartz and Israel Scheffler. Our joint report was published in the *Journal of Philosophy*, volume 67 (1970), pages 605 through 608, under the title "An Improvement in the Theory of Projectibility".

In the rather extensive discussion relating to this book, some interesting points have been made. Scheffler's examination of selective confirmation paved the way for Marsha Hanen's convincing argument that all the familiar so-called adequacy conditions for confirmation are dispensable. Wolfgang Stegmüller has corrected the notion that 'anti-inductivists' of the school of Karl Popper escape the new riddle of induction. Elizabeth Shipley has quite justly remarked that along with number of projections, such other factors as the importance, variety, and Humean 'liveliness' of the projections contribute to the entrenchment of a predicate. Other writers have noted additional defects in the attempt to delimit the relevant conditions for counterfactuals; but since that attempt is here (I.2) rejected anyway on other grounds, further flaws are of minor interest. Some brief reservations and clarifications carried over from the second edition resulted from discussions with Scheffler, C. G. Hempel, and Howard Kahane. Kahane indeed deserves special, if left-handed, credit. Ironically, his persistent efforts to demolish the whole theory of projectibility by counterexample have instead shown that this admittedly tentative and fragmentary theory is, with some modifications and simplications, more nearly adequate and more durable than I had supposed.

Among the most common mistakes in discussions of this book have been failures to recognize (1) that the projectibility status of a hypothesis normally varies from time to time, (2) that even an emerald existing from prehistoric time may be grue while remaining green, (3) that a major obstacle to a nonpragmatic way of ruling out 'grue-like' predicates is the lack of any non-question-begging definition of "grue-like", (4) that the discussion of possibility in Chapter II is concerned not with the question raised when we say that something may or may not be in fact a soandso but with the question raised when we say that something that is not in fact a soandso is nevertheless a possible soandso, (5) that since at any time as many supported, unviolated, and unexhausted hypotheses are not projectible as are projectible, projectible hypotheses or predicates cannot be defined in terms of survival of the fittest, and (6) that the analogy I have drawn between justification of induction and justification of deduction is quite independent of the obvious fact that, when valid, deductive but not inductive inference always yields a true conclusion from true premisses.

Some of these matters, both positive and negative, have been discussed a little more fully in my *Problems and Projects* (Bobbs-Merrill, 1972, Chapter VIII), but could not be incorporated in the present text.

In addition to the important improvement mentioned above, several minor revisions have been made in this edition, and a new index has been prepared by Samuel Scheffler.

Nelson Goodman

Harvard University
March 1973

INTRODUCTION

The chapters to follow were all originally delivered as lectures. Although seven years and a few thousand miles separated the delivery of the first from the delivery of the remaining three, the four represent a consecutive effort of thought on a closely integrated group of problems. Only the first has been published before.

In the summer of 1944, I had nearly completed a manuscript entitled 'Two Essays on Not-Being'. The first essay explained the counterfactual conditional, and the second made use of this explanation in dealing with potentiality, possibility, and dispositions. Some minor difficulties in the first essay still needed attention, however, and these led to less minor ones until, a few weeks later, my two essays were instances rather than treatments of not-being.

Grasping at the scientist's slim straw of solace, that failure is as significant as success, I used the detailed history of this frustration as the subject for a talk given in New York in May of 1946. It was published a few months later in the *Journal of Philosophy* as 'The Problem of Counterfactual Conditionals'.

The scores of articles that have been published since then have made so little progress towards settling the matter that current opinion varies all the way from the view that the problem is no problem at all to the view that it is insoluble. Neither of these extremes is very well substantiated. The former is usually supported by the claim that we can, theoretically at least, get along without counterfactuals in the sciences. But however that may be, we do not yet by any means know how to get along without them (or transparent substitutes for them) in philosophy. The view that the problem is insoluble is sometimes supported by the citation of paradoxical counterfactuals that confound commonsense. But such cases do not argue insolubility; for if we can provide an interpretation that handles the clear cases successfully, we can let the unclear ones fall where they may.

The urge to dispose of the problem as spurious or insoluble is understandable, of course, in view of the repeated failures to find a solution. The trouble is, though, that what confronts us is not a single isolated problem but a closely knit family of problems. If we set one of them aside, we usually encounter much the same difficulties when we try to deal with the others. And if we set aside all the problems of dispositions, possibility, scientific law, confirmation, and the like, we virtually abandon the philosophy of science.

For some years, work on a book dealing with other matters took most of my time; but after *The Structure of Appearance* was published in 1951, I turned again to the problem of counterfactuals and kindred problems—and began to travel in all the old circles. When, in 1952, the University of London invited me to give some lectures the following year, I set to work with a conviction that some new approach must be found. The results of that work were reported in three lectures delivered in London in May of 1953 under the general title *Fact, Fiction, and Forecast.*

In the present book, the first part 'Predicament—1946' consists of 'The Problem of Counterfactual Conditionals', reprinted without major changes. The second part 'Project—1953' consists of the three London lectures now printed for the first time. These have been somewhat revised, and rather extensive notes have been added. The greatest change, involving many additions and improvements, has occurred in the expansion of the last quarter of the final lecture into the last half of the fourth chapter. I am indebted to C. G. Hempel for many useful suggestions, and to Elizabeth F. Flower for valuable editorial assistance.

The two parts of the book are intimately related to each other in the ways I have described; but no attempt has been made to revise them to make a more continuous whole. The occasional duplications and minor disparities between the work of 1946 and the work of 1953 have been left untouched. Thus readers familiar with the article on counterfactuals or unready for its technicalities will find the second part a more or less self-contained unit, while other readers will find in the first part an essentially unaltered description of the state of affairs from which the London lectures took their departure. The layman and the beginning student may well read the second part first.

Throughout I have used commonplace and even trivial illustrations rather than more intriguing ones drawn from the sciences; for I feel that examples that attract the least interest to themselves are the least likely to divert attention from the problem or principle being explained. Once the reader has grasped a point he can make his own more consequential applications. Thus although I talk of the freezing of radiators and the color of marbles, which are seldom discussed in books on chemistry or physics, what I am saying falls squarely within the philosophy of science.

As yet we are able to deal with only a few aspects of a few problems. We have to isolate for study a few simple aspects of science just as science has to isolate a few simple aspects of the world; and we are at an even more rudimentary stage in philosophy than in science. This, admittedly, is over-simplification. But conscious and cautious over-simplification, far from being an intellectual sin, is a prerequisite for investigation. We can hardly study at once all the ways in which everything is related to everything else.

Four lectures do not make a treatise. This is a report of work in process that I hope may prove to be work in progress. It might be thought of as consisting of first thoughts towards a far-off sequel to *The Structure of Appearance*. But no acquaintance with that book, and no knowledge of symbolic logic, is required for an understanding of the present work.

Fact, Fiction, and Forecast

Third Edition

PREDICAMENT

1946

The chapter to follow was originally delivered as a lecture at the New York Philosophical Circle on May 11, 1946; and published with some revisions in the Journal of Philosophy *in February 1947, volume xliv, pages 113–28. Only minor changes have been made in the present text.*

I

THE PROBLEM OF COUNTERFACTUAL CONDITIONALS[1]

1. The Problem in General

The analysis of counterfactual conditionals is no fussy little grammatical exercise. Indeed, if we lack the means for interpreting counterfactual conditionals, we can hardly claim to have any adequate philosophy of science. A satisfactory definition of scientific law, a satisfactory theory of confirmation or of disposition terms (and this includes not only predicates ending in "ible" and "able" but almost every objective predicate, such as "is red"), would solve a large part of the problem of counterfactuals. Conversely, a solution to the problem of counterfactuals would give us the answer to critical questions about law, confirmation, and the meaning of potentiality.

I am not at all contending that the problem of counterfactuals is logically or psychologically the first of these related problems. It makes little difference where we start if we can go ahead. If the study of counterfactuals has up to now failed this pragmatic test, the alternative approaches are little better off.

---

[1] My indebtedness in several matters to the work of C. I. Lewis has seemed too obvious to call for detailed mention.

What, then, is the *problem* about counterfactual conditionals? Let us confine ourselves to those in which antecedent and consequent are inalterably false—as, for example, when I say of a piece of butter that was eaten yesterday, and that had never been heated,

If that piece of butter had been heated to 150° F., it would have melted.

Considered as truth-functional compounds, all counterfactuals are of course true, since their antecedents are false. Hence

If that piece of butter had been heated to 150° F., it would not have melted

would also hold. Obviously something different is intended, and the problem is to define the circumstances under which a given counterfactual holds while the opposing conditional with the contradictory consequent fails to hold. And this criterion of truth must be set up in the face of the fact that a counterfactual by its nature can never be subjected to any direct empirical test by realizing its antecedent.

In one sense the name "problem of counterfactuals" is misleading, because the problem is independent of the form in which a given statement happens to be expressed. The problem of counterfactuals is equally a problem of factual conditionals, for any counterfactual can be transposed into a conditional with a true antecedent and consequent; e.g.,

Since that butter did not melt, it wasn't heated to 150° F.

The possibility of such transformation is of no great importance except to clarify the nature of our problem. That

4

"since" occurs in the contrapositive shows that what is in question is a certain kind of connection between the two component sentences; and the truth of statements of this kind—whether they have the form of counterfactual or factual conditionals or some other form—depends not upon the truth or falsity of the components but upon whether the intended connection obtains. Recognizing the possibility of transformation serves mainly to focus attention on the central problem and to discourage speculation as to the nature of counterfacts. Although I shall begin my study by considering counterfactuals as such, it must be borne in mind that a general solution would explain the kind of connection involved irrespective of any assumption as to the truth or falsity of the components.

The effect of transposition upon conditionals of another kind, which I call "semifactuals", is worth noticing briefly. Should we assert

Even if the match had been scratched, it still would not have lighted,

we would uncompromisingly reject as an equally good expression of our meaning the contrapositive,

Even if the match lighted, it still wasn't scratched.

Our original intention was to affirm not that the non-lighting could be inferred from the scratching, but simply that the lighting could not be inferred from the scratching. Ordinarily a semifactual conditional has the force of denying what is affirmed by the opposite, fully counterfactual conditional. The sentence

Even had that match been scratched, it still wouldn't have lighted is normally meant as the direct negation of

Had the match been scratched, it would have lighted.

That is to say, in practice full counterfactuals affirm, while semifactuals deny, that a certain connection obtains between antecedent and consequent.[2] Thus it is clear why a semifactual generally has not the same meaning as its contrapositive.

There are various special kinds of counterfactuals that present special problems. An example is the case of 'counteridenticals', illustrated by the statements

If I were Julius Caesar, I wouldn't be alive in the twentieth century,

and

If Julius Caesar were I, he would be alive in the twentieth century.

Here, although the antecedent in the two cases is a statement of the same identity, we attach two different consequents which, on the very assumption of that identity, are incompatible. Another special class of counterfactuals is that of the 'countercomparatives', with antecedents such as

If I had more money, ...

The trouble with these is that when we try to translate the counterfactual into a statement about a relation between

---

[2] The practical import of a semifactual is thus different from its literal import. Literally a semifactual and the corresponding counterfactual are not contradictories but contraries, and both may be false (cf. Note I.9 below). The presence of the auxiliary terms "even" and "still", or either of them, is perhaps the idiomatic indication that a not quite literal meaning is intended.

two tenseless, non-modal sentences, we get as an antecedent something like

If "I have more money than I have" were true, . . . ,

which wrongly represents the original antecedent as self-contradictory. Again there are the 'counterlegals', conditionals with antecedents that either deny general laws directly, as in

If triangles were squares, . . . ,

or else make a supposition of particular fact that is not merely false but impossible, as in

If this cube of sugar were also spherical, ...

Counterfactuals of all these kinds offer interesting but not insurmountable special difficulties.[3] In order to concentrate upon the major problems concerning counterfactuals in general, I shall usually choose my examples in such a way as to avoid these more special complications.

As I see it, there are two major problems, though they are not independent and may even be regarded as aspects of a single problem. A counterfactual is true if a certain connection obtains between the antecedent and the con-

---

[3] Of the special kinds of counterfactuals mentioned, I shall have something to say later about counteridenticals and counterlegals. As for countercomparatives, the following procedure is appropriate:—Given "If I had arrived one minute later, I would have missed the train", first expand this to "I arrived at a given time. If I had arrived one minute later than that, I would have missed the train". The counterfactual conditional constituting the final clause of this conjunction can then be treated in the usual way. Translation into "If 'I arrive one minute later than the given time' were true, then 'I miss the train' would have been true" does not give us a self-contradictory component.

sequent. But as is obvious from examples already given, the consequent seldom follows from the antecedent by logic alone. (1) In the first place, the assertion that a connection holds is made on the presumption that certain circumstances not stated in the antecedent obtain. When we say

If that match had been scratched, it would have lighted,

we mean that conditions are such—i.e. the match is well made, is dry enough, oxygen enough is present, etc.—that "That match lights" can be inferred from "That match is scratched". Thus the connection we affirm may be regarded as joining the consequent with the conjunction of the antecedent and other statements that truly describe relevant conditions. Notice especially that our assertion of the counterfactual is *not* conditioned upon these circumstances obtaining. We do not assert that the counterfactual is true *if* the circumstances obtain; rather, in asserting the counterfactual we commit ourselves to the actual truth of the statements describing the requisite relevant conditions. The first major problem is to define relevant conditions: to specify what sentences are meant to be taken in conjunction with an antecedent as a basis for inferring the consequent. (2) But even after the particular relevant conditions are specified, the connection obtaining will not ordinarily be a logical one. The principle that permits inference of

That match lights

from

That match is scratched. That match is dry enough. Enough oxygen is present. Etc.

8

is not a law of logic but what we call a natural or physical or causal law. The second major problem concerns the definition of such laws.

2. *The Problem of Relevant Conditions*

It might seem natural to propose that the consequent follows by law from the antecedent and a description of the actual state-of-affairs of the world, that we need hardly define relevant conditions because it will do no harm to include irrelevant ones. But if we say that the consequent follows by law from the antecedent and *all* true statements, we encounter an immediate difficulty:— among true sentences is the negate of the antecedent, so that from the antecedent and all true sentences everything follows. Certainly this gives us no way of distinguishing true from false counterfactuals.

We are plainly no better off if we say that the consequent must follow from *some* set of true statements conjoined with the antecedent; for given any counterfactual antecedent *A*, there will always be a set *S*—namely, the set consisting of *not-A*—such that from *A·S* any consequent follows. (Hereafter I shall regularly use the following symbols: "*A*" for the antecedent; "*C*" for the consequent; "*S*" for the set of statements of the relevant conditions or, indifferently, for the conjunction of these statements.)

Perhaps then we must exclude statements logically incompatible with the antecedent. But this is insufficient; for a parallel difficulty arises with respect to true statements which are not logically but are otherwise incompatible with the antecedent. For example, take

If that radiator had frozen, it would have broken.

Among true sentences may well be (*S*)

That radiator never reached a temperature below 33° F.

Now we have as true generalizations both

All radiators that freeze but never reach below 33° F. break,

and also

All radiators that freeze but never reach below 33° F. fail to break;

for there are no such radiators. Thus from the antecedent of the counterfactual and the given *S*, we can infer any consequent.

The natural proposal to remedy this difficulty is to rule that counterfactuals cannot depend upon empty laws; that the connection can be established only by a principle of the form "All *x*'s are *y*'s" when there are some *x*'s. But this is ineffectual. For if empty principles are excluded, the following non-empty principles may be used in the case given with the same result:

Everything that is either a radiator that freezes but does not reach below 33° F., or that is a soap bubble, breaks;

Everything that is either a radiator that freezes but does not reach below 33° F., or is powder, does not break.

By these principles we can infer any consequent from the *A* and *S* in question.

The only course left open to us seems to be to define relevant conditions as the set of all true statements each of which is both logically and non-logically compatible with *A* where non-logical incompatibility means violation of a non-logical law.[4] But another difficulty immediately appears. In a counterfactual beginning

If Jones were in Carolina, . . .

the antecedent is entirely compatible with

Jones is not in South Carolina

and with

Jones is not in North Carolina

and with

North Carolina plus South Carolina is identical with Carolina;

but all these taken together with the antecedent make a set that is self-incompatible, so that again any consequent would be forthcoming.

Clearly it will not help to require only that for *some* set S of true sentences, A·S be self-compatible and lead by law to the consequent; for this would make a true counterfactual of

If Jones were in Carolina, he would be in South Carolina,

and also of

If Jones were in Carolina, he would be in North Carolina,

which cannot both be true.

It seems that we must elaborate our criterion still further, to characterize a counterfactual as true if and only if there is some set S of true statements such that A·S is self-compatible and leads by law to the consequent, while there

---

[4] This of course raises very serious questions, which I shall come to presently, about the nature of non-logical law.

is no such set S' such that $A \cdot S'$ is self-compatible and leads by law to the negate of the consequent.[5] Unfortunately even this is not enough. For among true sentences will be the negate of the consequent: $-C$. Is $-C$ compatible with A or not? If not, then A alone without any additional conditions must lead by law to C. But if $-C$ is compatible with A (as in most cases), then if we take $-C$ as our S, the conjunction $A \cdot S$ will give us $-C$. Thus the criterion we have set up will seldom be satisfied; for since $-C$ will normally be compatible with A, as the need for introducing the relevant conditions testifies, there will normally be an S (namely, $-C$) such that $A \cdot S$ is self-compatible and leads by law to $-C$.

Part of our trouble lies in taking too narrow a view of our problem. We have been trying to lay down conditions under which an A that is known to be false leads to a C that is known to be false; but it is equally important to make sure that our criterion does not establish a similar connection between our A and the (true) negate of C. Because our S together with A was to be so chosen as to give us C, it seemed gratuitous to specify that S must be compatible with C; and because $-C$ is true by supposition, S would necessarily be compatible with it. But we are testing whether our criterion not only admits the true counterfactual we are concerned with but also excludes the

---

[5] Note that the requirement that $A \cdot S$ be self-compatible can be fulfilled only if the antecedent is self-compatible; hence the conditionals I have called "counterlegals" will all be false. This is convenient for our present purpose of investigating counterfactuals that are not counterlegals. If it later appears desirable to regard all or some counterlegals as true, special provisions may be introduced.

opposing conditional. Accordingly, our criterion must be modified by specifying that S be compatible with both C and $-C$.[6] In other words, S by itself must not decide between C and $-C$, but S together with A must lead to C but not to $-C$. We need not know whether C is true or false.

Our rule thus reads that a counterfactual is true if and only if there is some set S of true sentences such that S is compatible with C and with $-C$, and such that $A \cdot S$ is self-compatible and leads by law to C; while there is no set S' compatible with C and with $-C$, and such that $A \cdot S'$ is self-compatible and leads by law to $-C$.[7] As thus stated, the rule involves a certain redundancy; but simplification is not in point here, for the criterion is still inadequate.

The requirement that $A \cdot S$ be self-compatible is not strong enough; for S might comprise true sentences that although *compatible with* A, were such that *they would*

---

[6] It is natural to inquire whether for similar reasons we should stipulate that S must be compatible with both A and $-A$, but this is unnecessary. For if S is incompatible with $-A$, then A follows from S; therefore if S is compatible with both C and $-C$, then $A \cdot S$ cannot lead by law to one but not the other. Hence no sentence incompatible with $-A$ can satisfy the other requirements for a suitable S.

[7] Since the first edition of this book, W. T. Parry has pointed out that no counterfactual satisfies this formula; for one can always take $-(A \cdot -C)$ as S, and take $-(A \cdot C)$ as S'. Thus we must add the requirement that neither S nor S' follows by law from $-A$. Of course this does not alleviate the further difficulties explained in the following paragraphs of the text above. (See Parry's 'Reexamination of the Problem of Counterfactual Conditionals', *Journal of Philosophy*, vol. 54 [1957], pp. 85–94, and my 'Parry on Counterfactuals', same journal, same volume, pp. 442–5.)

not be true if A were true. For this reason, many statements that we would regard as definitely false would be true according to the stated criterion. As an example, consider the familiar case where for a given match m, we would affirm

(i) If match m had been scratched, it would have lighted,

but deny

(ii) If match m had been scratched, it would not have been dry.[8]

According to our tentative criterion, statement (ii) would be quite as true as statement (i). For in the case of (ii), we may take as an element in our S the true sentence

Match m did not light,

which is presumably compatible with A (otherwise nothing would be required along with A to reach the opposite as the consequent of the true counterfactual statement (i)). As our total $A \cdot S$ we may have

Match m is scratched. It does not light. It is well made. Oxygen enough is present . . . etc.;

and from this, by means of a legitimate general law, we can infer

It was not dry.

And there would seem to be no suitable set of sentences S' such that $A \cdot S'$ leads by law to the negate of this conse-

---

[8] Of course, some sentences similar to (ii), referring to other matches under special conditions, may be true; but the objection to the proposed criterion is that it would commit us to many such statements that are patently false. I am indebted to Morton G. White for a suggestion concerning the exposition of this point.

quent. Hence the unwanted counterfactual is established in accord with our rule. The trouble is caused by including in our S a true statement which though compatible with A would not be true if A were. Accordingly we must exclude such statements from the set of relevant conditions; S, in addition to satisfying the other requirements already laid down, must be not merely compatible with A but 'jointly tenable' or *cotenable* with A. A is cotenable with S, and the conjunction $A·S$ self-cotenable, if it is not the case that S would not be true if A were.[9]

Parenthetically it may be noted that the relative fixity of conditions is often unclear, so that the speaker or writer has to make explicit additional provisos or give subtle verbal clues as to his meaning. For example, each of the following two counterfactuals would normally be accepted:

If New York City were in Georgia, then New York City would be in the South.

If Georgia included New York City, then Georgia would not be entirely in the South.

Yet the antecedents are logically indistinguishable. What happens is that the direction of expression becomes important, because in the former case the meaning is

---

[9] The double negative cannot be eliminated here; for "... if S would be true if A were" actually constitutes a stronger requirement. As we noted earlier (Note I.2), if two conditionals having the same counterfactual antecedent are such that the consequent of one is the negate of the consequent of the other, the conditionals are contraries and both may be false. This will be the case, for example, if every otherwise suitable set of relevant conditions that in conjunction with the antecedent leads by law either to a given consequent or its negate leads also to the other.

If New York City were in Georgia, and the boundaries of
Georgia remained unchanged, then . . . ,

while in the latter case the meaning is

If Georgia included New York City, and the boundaries of
New York City remained unchanged, then . . . .

Without some such cue to the meaning as is covertly given
by the word-order, we should be quite uncertain which of
the two consequents in question could be truly attached.
The same kind of explanation accounts for the paradoxical
pairs of counteridenticals mentioned earlier.

Returning now to the proposed rule, I shall neither offer
further corrections of detail nor discuss whether the requirement that S be cotenable with A makes superfluous
some other provisions of the criterion; for such matters
become rather unimportant beside the really serious difficulty that now confronts us. In order to determine the
truth of a given counterfactual it seems that we have to
determine, among other things, whether there is a suitable
S that is cotenable with A and meets certain further requirements. But in order to determine whether or not a
given S is cotenable with A, we have to determine whether
or not the counterfactual "If A were true, then S would
not be true" is itself true. But this means determining
whether or not there is a suitable S_1, cotenable with A, that
leads to $-S$ and so on. Thus we find ourselves involved in
an infinite regressus or a circle; for cotenability is defined
in terms of counterfactuals, yet the meaning of counterfactuals is defined in terms of cotenability. In other words
to establish any counterfactual, it seems that we first have
to determine the truth of another. If so, we can never
explain a counterfactual except in terms of others, so that

the problem of counterfactuals must remain unsolved.

Though unwilling to accept this conclusion, I do not at present see any way of meeting the difficulty. One naturally thinks of revising the whole treatment of counterfactuals in such a way as to admit first those that depend on no conditions other than the antecedent, and then use these counterfactuals as the criteria for the cotenability of relevant conditions with antecedents of other counterfactuals, and so on. But this idea seems initially rather unpromising in view of the formidable difficulties of accounting by such a step-by-step method for even so simple a counterfactual as

If the match had been scratched, it would have lighted.

3. The Problem of Law

Even more serious is the second of the problems mentioned earlier: the nature of the general statements that enable us to infer the consequent upon the basis of the antecedent and the statement of relevant conditions. The distinction between these connecting principles and relevant conditions is imprecise and arbitrary; the 'connecting principles' might be conjoined to the condition-statements, and the relation of the antecedent-conjunction $(A \cdot S)$ to the consequent thus made a matter of logic. But the same problems would arise as to the kind of principle that is capable of sustaining a counterfactual; and it is convenient to consider the connecting principles separately.

In order to infer the consequent of a counterfactual from the antecedent A and a suitable statement of relevant conditions S, we make use of a general statement; namely, the generalization[10] of the conditional having $A \cdot S$ for antecedent and C for consequent. For example, in the case of

If the match had been scratched, it would have lighted

the connecting principle is

Every match that is scratched, well made, dry enough, in enough oxygen, etc., lights.

But notice that *not* every counterfactual is actually sustained by the principle thus arrived at, *even* if that principle is *true*. Suppose, for example, that all I had in my right pocket on VE day was a group of silver coins. Now we would not under normal circumstances affirm of a given penny P

If P had been in my pocket on VE day, P would have been silver,[11]

even though from

P was in my pocket on VE day

---

[10] The sense of "generalization" intended here is that explained by C. G. Hempel in 'A Purely Syntactical Definition of Confirmation', *Journal of Symbolic Logic*, vol. 8 (1943), pp. 122–43. See also III.3, below.

[11] The antecedent in this example is intended to mean "If P, while remaining distinct from the things that were in fact in my pocket on VE day, had also been in my pocket then", and *not* the quite different, counteridentical "If P had been identical with one of the things that were in my pocket on VE day". While the antecedents of most counterfactuals (as, again, our familiar one about the match) are—literally speaking—open to both sorts of interpretation, ordinary usage normally calls for some explicit indication when the counteridentical meaning is intended.

we can infer the consequent by means of the general statement

Everything in my pocket on VE day was silver.

On the contrary, we would assert that if P had been in my pocket, then this general statement would not be true. The general statement will *not* permit us to infer the given consequent from the counterfactual assumption that P was in my pocket, because the general statement will not itself withstand that counterfactual assumption. Though the supposed connecting principle is indeed general, true, and perhaps even fully confirmed by observation of all cases, it is incapable of sustaining a counterfactual because it remains a description of accidental fact, not a law. The truth of a counterfactual conditional thus seems to depend on whether the general sentence required for the inference is a law or not. If so, our problem is to distinguish accurately between causal laws and casual facts.[12]

The problem illustrated by the example of the coins is closely related to that which led us earlier to require the cotenability of the antecedent and the relevant conditions, in order to avoid resting a counterfactual on any statement that would not be true if the antecedent were true. For decision as to the cotenability of two sentences depends partly upon decisions as to whether certain general statements are laws, and we are now concerned directly with

---

[12] The importance of distinguishing laws from non-laws is too often overlooked. If a clear distinction can be defined, it may serve not only the purposes explained in the present paper but also many of those for which the increasingly dubious distinction between analytic and synthetic statements is ordinarily supposed to be needed.

the latter problem. Is there some way of so distinguishing laws from non-laws, among true universal statements of the kind in question, that laws will be the principles that will sustain counterfactual conditionals?

Any attempt to draw the distinction by reference to a notion of causative force can be dismissed at once as unscientific. And it is clear that no purely syntactical criterion can be adequate, for even the most special descriptions of particular facts can be cast in a form having any desired degree of syntactical universality. "Book B is small" becomes "Everything that is Q is small" if "Q" stands for some predicate that applies uniquely to B. What then does distinguish a law like

All butter melts at 150° F.

from a true and general non-law like

All the coins in my pocket are silver ?

Primarily, I would like to suggest, the fact that the first is accepted as true while many cases of it remain to be determined, the further, unexamined cases being predicted to conform with it. The second sentence, on the contrary, is accepted as a description of contingent fact *after* the determination of all cases, no prediction of any of its instances being based upon it. This proposal raises innumerable problems, some of which I shall consider presently; but the idea behind it is just that the principle we use to decide counterfactual cases is a principle we are willing to commit ourselves to in deciding unrealized cases that are still subject to direct observation.

As a first approximation then, we might say that a law is a true sentence used for making predictions. That laws are used predictively is of course a simple truism, and I am not proposing it as a novelty. I want only to emphasize the Humean idea that rather than a sentence being used for prediction because it is a law, it is called a law because it is used for prediction; and that rather than the law being used for prediction because it describes a causal connection, the meaning of the causal connection is to be interpreted in terms of predictively used laws.

By the determination of all instances, I mean simply the examination or testing by other means of all things that satisfy the antecedent, to decide whether all satisfy the consequent also. There are difficult questions about the meaning of "instance", many of which Professor Hempel has investigated. Most of these are avoided in our present study by the fact that we are concerned with a very narrow class of sentences: those arrived at by generalizing conditionals of a certain kind. Remaining problems about the meaning of "instance" I shall have to ignore here. As for "determination", I do not mean final discovery of truth, but only enough examination to reach a decision as to whether a given statement or its negate is to be admitted as evidence for the hypothesis in question.

Our criterion excludes vacuous principles as laws. The generalizations needed for sustaining counterfactual conditionals cannot be vacuous, for they must be supported by evidence.[13] The limited scope of our present problem

---

[13] Had it been sufficient in the preceding section to require only that $A \cdot S$ be self-*compatible*, this requirement might now be eliminated in favor of the stipulation that the generalization of the conditional having $A \cdot S$ as antecedent and C as consequent should be non-vacuous; but this stipulation would not guarantee the self-*cotenability* of $A \cdot S$.

makes it unimportant that our criterion, if applied generally to all statements, would classify as laws many statements—e.g., true singular predictions—that we would not normally call laws.

For convenience, I shall use the term "lawlike" for sentences that, whether they are true or not, satisfy the other requirements in the definition of law. A law is thus a sentence that is both lawlike and true, but a sentence may be true without being lawlike, as I have illustrated, or lawlike without being true, as we are always learning to our dismay.

Now if we were to leave our definition as it stands, lawlikeness would be a rather accidental and ephemeral property. Only statements that happen actually to have been used for prediction would be lawlike. And a true sentence that had been used predictively would cease to be a law when it became fully tested—i.e., when none of its instances remained undetermined. The definition, then, must be restated in some such way as this: A general statement is lawlike if and only if it is acceptable prior to the determination of all its instances. This is immediately objectionable because "acceptable" itself is plainly a dispositional term; but I propose to use it only tentatively, with the idea of eliminating it eventually by means of a nondispositional definition. Before trying to accomplish that, however, we must face another difficulty in our tentative criterion of lawlikeness.

Suppose that the appropriate generalization fails to sustain a given counterfactual because that generalization, while true, is unlawlike, as is

Everything in my pocket is silver.

All we would need to do to get a law would be to broaden the antecedent strategically. Consider, for example, the sentence

Everything that is in my pocket or is a dime is silver.

Since we have not examined all dimes, this is a predictive statement and—since presumably true—would be a law. Now if we consider our original counterfactual and choose our S so that $A \cdot S$ is

P is in my pocket. P is in my pocket or is a dime,

then the pseudo-law just constructed can be used to infer from this the sentence "P is silver". Thus the untrue counterfactual is established. If one prefers to avoid an alternation as a condition-statement, the same result can be obtained by using a new predicate such as "dimo" to mean "is in my pocket or is a dime".[14]

The change called for, I think, will make the definition of lawlikeness read as follows: A sentence is lawlike if its acceptance does not depend upon the determination of any given instance.[15] Naturally this does not mean that

---

[14] Apart from the special class of connecting principles we are concerned with, note that under the stated criterion of lawlikeness, any statement could be expanded into a lawlike one; for example: given "This book is black" we could use the predictive sentence "This book is black and all oranges are spherical" to argue that the blackness of the book is the consequence of a law.

[15] So stated, the definition counts vacuous principles as laws. If we read instead "given class of instances", vacuous principles will be non-laws since their acceptance depends upon examination of the null class of instances. For my present purposes the one formulation is as good as the other.

acceptance is to be independent of all determination of instances, but only that there is no particular instance on the determination of which acceptance depends. This criterion excludes from the class of laws a statement like

That book is black and oranges are spherical

on the ground that acceptance requires knowing whether the book is black; it excludes

Everything that is in my pocket or is a dime is silver

on the ground that acceptance demands examination of all things in my pocket. Moreover, it excludes a statement like

All the marbles in this bag except Number 19 are red, and Number 19 is black

on the ground that acceptance would depend on examination of or knowledge gained otherwise concerning marble Number 19. In fact the principle involved in the proposed criterion is a rather powerful one and seems to exclude most of the troublesome cases.

We must still, however, replace the notion of the acceptability of a sentence, or of its acceptance *depending* or *not depending* on some given knowledge, by a positive definition of such dependence. It is clear that to say that the acceptance of a given statement depends upon a certain kind and amount of evidence is to say that given such evidence, acceptance of the statement is in accord with certain general standards for the acceptance of statements that are not fully tested. So one turns naturally to theories of induction and confirmation to learn the distinguishing factors or circumstances that determine whether or not a sentence is acceptable without complete evidence. But publications on confirmation not only have failed to make clear the distinction between confirmable and non-confirmable statements, but show little recognition that such a problem exists.[16] Yet obviously in the case of some sentences like

Everything in my pocket is silver

or

No twentieth-century president of the United States will be between 6 feet 1 inch and 6 feet 1½ inches tall,

not even the testing with positive results of all but a single instance is likely to lead us to accept the sentence and predict that the one remaining instance will conform to it; while for other sentences such as

All dimes are silver

or

All butter melts at 150° F.

or

All flowers of plants descended from this seed will be yellow,

positive determination of even a few instances may lead us to accept the sentence with confidence and make predictions in accordance with it.

There is some hope that cases like these can be dealt with by a sufficiently careful and intricate elaboration of current confirmation theories; but inattention to the problem

---

[16] The points discussed in this and the following paragraph have been dealt with a little more fully in my 'A Query on Confirmation', *Journal of Philosophy*, vol. xliii (1946), pp. 383–5.

of distinguishing between confirmable and non-confirmable sentences has left most confirmation theories open to more damaging counterexamples of an elementary kind.

Suppose we designate the 26 marbles in a bag by the letters of the alphabet, using these merely as proper names having no ordinal significance. Suppose further that we are told that all the marbles except d are red, but we are not told what color d is. By the usual kind of confirmation theory this gives strong confirmation for the statement

Ra. Rb. Rc. Rd. . . . Rz

because 25 of the 26 cases are known to be favorable while none is known to be unfavorable. But unfortunately the same argument would show that the very same evidence would equally confirm

Ra. Rb. Rc. Re. . . . Rz. —Rd,

for again we have 25 favorable and no unfavorable cases. Thus "Rd" and "—Rd" are equally and strongly confirmed by the same evidence. If I am required to use a single predicate instead of both "R" and "—R" in the second case, I will use "P" to mean:

is in the bag and either is not d and is red, or is d and is not red.

Then the evidence will be 25 positive cases for

All the marbles are P

from which it follows that d is P, and thus that d is not red. The problem of what statements are confirmable merely becomes the equivalent problem of what predicates are projectible from known to unknown cases.

So far, I have discovered no way of meeting these difficulties. Yet as we have seen, some solution is urgently wanted for our present purpose; for only where willingness to accept a statement involves predictions of instances that may be tested does acceptance endow that statement with the authority to govern counterfactual cases, which cannot be directly tested.

In conclusion, then, some problems about counterfactuals depend upon the definition of cotenability, which in turn seems to depend upon the prior solution of those problems. Other problems require an adequate definition of law. The tentative criterion of law here proposed is reasonably satisfactory in excluding unwanted kinds of statements, and in effect, reduces one aspect of our problem to the question how to define the circumstances under which a statement is acceptable independently of the determination of any given instance. But this question I do not know how to answer.

PROJECT

1953

The three chapters to follow are somewhat revised versions of the Special Lectures in Philosophy delivered at the University of London on May 21, 26 and 28, 1953. The first of the three was repeated at Harvard University on December 2 of the same year. All are now published for the first time. The general Introduction to this book (pp. ix–xii) contains some remarks on the relationship between these three chapters and the preceding one.

II

THE PASSING OF THE POSSIBLE

1. Foreword: On the Philosophic Conscience

In life our problems often result from our indulgences; in philosophy they derive rather from our abnegations. Yet if life is not worthwhile without its enjoyments, philosophy hardly exists without its restraints. A philosophic problem is a call to provide an adequate explanation in terms of an acceptable basis. If we are ready to tolerate everything as understood, there is nothing left to explain; while if we sourly refuse to take anything, even tentatively, as clear, no explanation can be given. What intrigues us as a problem, and what will satisfy us as a solution, will depend upon the line we draw between what is already clear and what needs to be clarified.

Yet I am afraid that we are nowhere near having any sound general principle for drawing this line. Surely I need not in this place and before this audience recount the tragic history of the verification theory of meaning.[1] The failure of this gallant effort to distinguish sense from nonsense,

---

[1] I allude here, of course, to A. J. Ayer's diligent but unsuccessful attempts to formulate the theory; see his *Language, Truth, and Logic*, London, 1946, pp. 5–16, 35–42. For a compact but comprehensive survey of the matter, see Hempel's article 'Problems and Changes in the Empiricist Criterion of Meaning' in *Revue Internationale de Philosophie*, vol. iv (1950), pp. 41–63. A verification

like the failure of various worthy efforts to codify the difference between right and wrong, has encouraged in some quarters the libertine doctrine that anything goes. The perverse maxim that whatever you can get away with is right has its counterpart in the claim that whatever works is clear. So crude a pragmatism deserves mention only because it seems to be spreading. I may not *understand* the devices I employ in making useful computations or predictions any more than the housewife understands the car she drives to bring home the groceries. The utility of a notion testifies not to its clarity but rather to the philosophic importance of clarifying it.

In the absence of any convenient and reliable criterion of what is clear, the individual thinker can only search his philosophic conscience. As is the way with consciences, it is elusive, variable, and too easily silenced in the face of hardship or temptation. At best it yields only specific judgments rather than general principles; and honest judgments made at different times or by different persons may differ in any degree. Indeed this talk of conscience is simply a figurative way of disclaiming any idea of justifying these basic judgments. Beyond making them carefully

---

criterion of meaningfulness was earnestly sought as a definitive basis for ruling out of court an immense amount of philosophical rubbish. But to find a formula that will do that without ruling out at the same time a good deal of perfectly respectable scientific theory has proved embarrassingly difficult. The disproportionate emphasis put on the problem has resulted in gross exaggeration of the consequences of the failure to solve it. Lack of a general theory of goodness does not turn vice into virtue; and lack of a general theory of significance does not turn empty verbiage into illuminating discourse.

and declaring them loudly, about all we can do is to disparage any alternatives. If your conscience is more liberal than mine, I shall call some of your explanations obscure or metaphysical, while you will dismiss some of my problems as trivial or quixotic.

All this is by way of preface to declaring that some of the things that seem to me inacceptable without explanation are powers or dispositions, counterfactual assertions, entities or experiences that are possible but not actual, neutrinos, angels, devils, and classes. Concerning the last of these, I have had a good deal to say elsewhere,[2] and I shall not press the point in these lectures. I shall use the language of classes rather freely because means have now been provided for giving a satisfactory interpretation of most ordinary statements about classes, and because I don't want to grind too many axes at once. Some other items on my list—angels and devils—enter so little into my daily discourse or into scientific discussions that I can wait patiently a long time for them to be explained. As for neutrinos and some other particles of physics, I think they are as yet beyond our philosophic reach. But the interrelated problems of dispositions, counterfactuals, and possibles are among the most urgent and most pervasive that confront us today in the theory of knowledge and the philosophy of science. It is this cluster of problems that I want to discuss in these lectures.

My sample listing of suspect notions is of course far from complete. Some of my other prejudices will be revealed by what I abjure in seeking a solution to the problems

---

[2] See my book *The Structure of Appearance*, 2d ed. (Indianapolis: The Bobbs-Merrill Company, Inc., 1966), Chapter II, Sections 2–3, and the articles there cited.

mentioned. For example, I shall not rely on the distinction between causal connections and accidental correlations, or on the distinction between essential and artificial kinds, or on the distinction between analytic and synthetic statements. You may decry some of these scruples and protest that there are more things in heaven and earth than are dreamt of in my philosophy. I am concerned, rather, that there should not be more things dreamt of in my philosophy than there are in heaven or earth.

Today let us examine briefly first the problem of counterfactuals, second the problem of dispositions, and finally the problem of possible entities. The reasons for this ordering will become apparent as we proceed.

2. Counterfactuals

A common habit of speech, a recent trend in philosophy, and the apparent ease of expressing in counterfactual form what we want to say about dispositions and possible entities make it natural to begin with the problem of counterfactual conditionals. Nowadays I think few of us are any longer willing to accept a counterfactual conditional, however impressively intoned, as providing in itself an explanation that requires no further analysis. The legal mind investigating the question what is meant by the value of real estate may rest content with the pronouncement that the value is the price the property would bring if it were sold by a willing seller to a willing buyer; but the philosopher (at least I) will regard this as reframing the question rather than answering it.

Nevertheless, replacement of a statement like

k was flexible at time t

34

by a statement like

If *k* had been under suitable pressure at time *t*, then *k* would have bent

has obvious promise as a step towards clarification. The disposition-term "flexible" is eliminated without the introduction of any such troublesome word as "possible"; only non-dispositional predicates appear to remain, even if they are slightly jaundiced with a modal inflection. Moreover, the counterfactual formulation seems already to effect at least a preliminary analysis, since a conditional is made up of simpler statements. Indeed, if we interpret the counterfactual conditional as saying

If the statement "*k* was under suitable pressure at time *t*" were true, then the statement "*k* bent at time *t*" would be true,

the modality is removed from the predicates and we may focus attention upon the relationship affirmed to hold between two simple indicative statements. By thus moving to the plane of relations between statements, we feel that we have exchanged an ontological problem for a linguistic one.[3] Also, we half-consciously expect that the truth-functional treatment of ordinary indicative conditionals will somehow serve as a helpful model for the analysis of counterfactuals. All these factors, I think—together with the prospect of acquiring at a single stroke the means for dealing with a whole tangle of problems—have contributed to a notable quickening of philosophical interest in the counterfactual conditional during the past few years.

---

[3] Cf. the discussion in Morton White's 'Ontological Clarity and Semantic Obscurity' in the *Journal of Philosophy*, vol. xlviii (1951), pp. 373–80.

Plainly, the truth-value of a counterfactual does not derive simply from the truth-value of its components; for since the antecedent and consequent of every counterfactual are both false,[4] all counterfactuals will have the same truth-value by any truth-functional criterion. Counterfactual connection must be defined in some quite different way. Some philosophers, of course, prefer to regard counterfactuals as rules or licenses for making inferences rather than as statements that are true or false. But whether we are seeking to distinguish true from false statements or distinguish valid from invalid licenses, the task is to discover the necessary and sufficient conditions under which counterfactual coupling of antecedent and consequent is warranted.

The relationship between the component statements of a true counterfactual is seldom a matter of logical implication. The statement

Match m lit at time t

does not follow by any familiar logical principle from the statement

Match m was scratched at time t;

there is an appeal to a general physical principle about matches. But two difficulties arise.

In the first place, matches do not always light when scratched. They light only if attendant circumstances are propitious. Let us, for easy reference, give the name "S" to the counterfactual statement

---

[4] Although I use the term "counterfactual" thus narrowly here, convenience is often served by including semifactuals—with false antecedents and true consequents—among the counterfactuals.

If *m* had been scratched at *t*, then *m* would have lit.

S does not merely affirm that if the circumstances had been propitious then the match would have lit; *S* affirms that the circumstances *were* propitious. A counterfactual is true if and only if the antecedent conjoined with relevant true statements about the attendant circumstances leads by way of a true general principle to the consequent. But what statements are relevant? Surely not, in the case of *S*, all true statements about *m* at *t*; for some of these (e.g "*m* was not scratched at *t*", and "*m* did not light at *t*") are incompatible with the antecedent or with the consequent. We soon find that other exclusions are needed; and after a long series of failures to arrive at a competent formula that is not itself counterfactual and therefore question-begging, we come to recognize that this aspect of the problem is very troublesome.[5]

In the second place, not every true general principle is capable of sustaining a counterfactual conditional. It is true that every person now in this room is safe from freezing. It is also true that every person now in this room is English-speaking. Now consider a certain Eskimo who is at this moment nearly frozen to death somewhere in the Arctic. If he were now in this room he would be safe from freezing, but he would not be English-speaking. What makes the difference? We may say that the generalization about safety from freezing expresses a causal relationship

---

[5] But it is often neglected in published discussions of counterfactuals. The problem of relevant conditions—most acutely felt as the problem of cotenability (see I.2)—does not, as some writers seem to suppose, reduce in any ready and obvious way to the problem of law.

or follows from a *law*, while the generalization about knowledge of English is only contingently or accidentally true; but to define this distinction is a delicate matter. Since we shall soon encounter the problem again, I shall go into no details at the moment; but this second aspect of the problem of counterfactuals, like the first, is formidable enough to have defied many intensive efforts to solve it.

These difficulties and the unsullied record of frustration in attempting to meet them have pretty thoroughly deflated our initial hope of finding a relatively easy approach to our problems through the study of the counterfactual conditional. We are still a very long way from having a solution to the problem of counterfactuals;[6] and by this time we may be ready to try another tack. After a number of years of beating our heads against the same wall and of chasing eagerly up the same blind alleys, we may welcome a change in strategy if only for its psychological benefits. But I think there are at least two better reasons for turning our attention for a while to the problem of dispositions.

First, in dealing with counterfactuals we are looking less at what is said than at the way it is said. We are expressly concerning ourselves with a *form* of statement; and the pattern of analysis we seek is largely dictated by

---

[6] I am not alone in this opinion. For example, Roderick Chisholm in a review in *Philosophy and Phenomenological Research* for September 1953 (vol. 14), p. 120, has just written concerning my article on counterfactuals: "It is safe to say, I think, that the extensive amount of material which has subsequently been published on this difficult philosophical problem has not thrown any additional light upon it."

the structure of the conditional. This structure, although it promised at the outset to be a valuable aid, may actually have become a hindrance. The very disanalysis effected by returning to consider dispositional statements, which are indicative and simple in form, may free us to explore a better scheme of analysis.

Second, I suspect that the problem of dispositions is really simpler than the problem of counterfactuals. This may sound strange in view of the apparent full convertibility between dispositional and counterfactual statements; but it turns out that ordinary dispositional statements often correspond to abnormally weak counterfactuals. Suppose that w is a piece of dry wood during a given brief period of time. We commonly suppose that a statement like

w is inflammable

amounts to some such normal counterfactual as

If w had been heated enough, it would have burned.

Once we look more closely, however, we can readily describe circumstances—for example, a lack of oxygen near w—under which the dispositional statement is true and the counterfactual false. For a translation guilty of no discrepancies like this we should be forced back to some such fainthearted counterfactual as

If all conditions had been propitious and w had been heated enough, it would have burned.

To speak very loosely, the dispositional statement says something exclusively about the 'internal state' of w, while our original counterfactual says in addition something about the surrounding circumstances; but the important point is that the dispositional statement is the weaker. And in the margin of difference may lie some of the obstacles that have blocked our way so far.

These, then, are some of the reasons for dropping the problem of counterfactuals for a time and seeing what can be done about the problem of dispositions; but I am by no means suggesting that this reorientation solves anything by itself or opens any royal road to progress.

3. Dispositions

Besides the observable properties it exhibits and the actual processes it undergoes, a thing is full of threats and promises. The dispositions or capacities of a thing—its flexibility, its inflammability, its solubility—are no less important to us than its overt behavior, but they strike us by comparison as rather ethereal. And so we are moved to inquire whether we can bring them down to earth; whether, that is, we can explain disposition-terms without any reference to occult powers.

Perhaps we ought to notice at the very beginning that more predicates than we sometimes suppose are dispositional. A tell-tale suffix like "ible" or "able" is not always present. To say that a thing is hard, quite as much as to say that it is flexible, is to make a statement about potentiality. If a flexible object is one capable of bending under appropriate pressure, a hard object is one capable of resisting abrasion by most other objects. And for that matter, a red object is likewise one capable of certain color-appearances under certain lights; and a cubical object is one capable of fitting try squares and measuring instruments in certain ways. Indeed, almost every predicate commonly thought of as describing a lasting objective characteristic of a thing is as much a dispositional predicate as any other. To find non-dispositional, or manifest, predicates of things we must turn to those describing events—predicates like "bends", "breaks", "burns", "dissolves", "looks orange", or "tests square". To apply such a predicate is to say that something specific actually happens with respect to the thing in question; while to apply a dispositional predicate is to speak only of what can happen.[7]

Now, however, we see that to put the problem of dispositions as a problem of explaining occult properties in terms of manifest ones is somewhat misleading. For even the manifest properties we have illustrated are hardly to be countenanced as elements of our universe. There are inflammable things and burning things but I should not want to say that there is any such entity as the attribute inflammable or the attribute burning. The predicate "burns" like the predicate "inflammable" is a word or label that applies to certain actual things and has the class of these things as its extension. Use of these predicates

---

[7] I have no illusion that this constitutes an adequate definition of the distinction between dispositional and manifest predicates. Indeed this distinction, like that between primitive and defined terms, may be a purely relative one. A predicate like "bends", for example, may be dispositional under a phenomenalistic system; and there may be no terms that are manifest—as there are no terms that are primitive—for all systems. The particular distinction drawn in the above text is thus perhaps best regarded as one chosen for the purpose of illustrating in a convenient and natural way the general problem of construing dispositional predicates on the basis of whatever predicates may be chosen as manifest.

does not imply that they designate attributive entities;[8] the predicates merely denote the things they apply to. A dispositional predicate, like a manifest predicate, is simply a term that applies to actual things; it need embrace no non-actuals in its extension.

The peculiarity of dispositional predicates is that they seem to be applied to things in virtue of possible rather than actual occurrences—and possible occurrences are for us no more admissible as unexplained elements than are occult capacities. The problem, then, is to explain how dispositional predicates can be assigned to things solely on the basis of actual occurrences and yet in due accordance with ordinary or scientific usage. In other words, what we want is a criterion in terms of actual occurrences—that is, in terms of manifest predicates—for the correct assignment of dispositional predicates to things.

The obvious first proposal is that a dispositional predicate is simply a summary description of certain aspects of the total history of a thing. Saying that an object is flexible is thus regarded as saying that it always bends whenever suitable pressure is applied. But the defects in this too-simple proposal are well-known. It results in ascribing flexibility to even the most rigid object that is never under

---

[8] Concerning the non-designative rôle of predicates, see various articles by W. V. Quine, most recently Essays I and II in his *From a Logical Point of View*, Cambridge (Mass.) and London, 1953. However, the reader's assent to Quine's views is not essential to my present purpose. I am primarily concerned above with pointing out that the problem about dispositional predicates does not arise from their failing to perform some designatory function that is performed by manifest predicates.

suitable pressure; for such an object bends on all those occasions (none) when it is under suitable pressure. And this proposal belies the fact that an object that is under suitable pressure at various times and bends at all such times may yet be inflexible at some other time when, for example, its temperature is very low. In short, a dispositional predicate may apply to a thing when the correlative manifest predicate does not apply at all. A thing that never bends may yet be flexible; an inflammable thing may happen never to burn.

The familiar and inevitable suggestion at this point is that a thing is flexible, even though it never bends, provided that it would bend if suitable pressure were applied. Then, however, we are no longer restricting ourselves to what actually happens but talking also of what fictively happens under certain possible conditions. Furthermore, we have seen that this way of translating dispositional statements is often inaccurate, and that anyhow no ground is gained by taking the problem of counterfactuals in trade for the problem of dispositions. Let us look for some more promising course.

In dealing with a particular disposition, say flexibility, we may start with such predicates as "bends" and "(is) under suitable pressure". If both apply at one time, then the predicate "bends under suitable pressure" applies; while if "under suitable pressure" applies when "bends" does not, then the predicate "fails to bend under suitable pressure" applies. For simplicity, we may take as our things not long-enduring physical objects but temporal segments of such objects brief enough so that none covers any two separate occasions when the object is under suitable pressure. We may also hereafter abbreviate "bends under suitable pressure" as "flexes" and "fails to bend under suitable pressure" as "fails to flex".

Now "flexes" and "fails to flex" are mutually exclusive, and together they exhaust the realm of things that are under suitable pressure; but neither applies to anything outside that realm. Thus from the fact that "flexes" does not apply to a thing, we cannot in general infer that "fails to flex" does apply. Within the realm of things under suitable pressure, however, the two predicates not only effect a dichotomy but coincide exactly with "flexible" and "inflexible". What the dispositional predicates do is, so to speak, to project this dichotomy to a wider or even to the universal class of things; and a predicate like "flexible" may thus be regarded as an expansion or projection of a predicate like "flexes". The problem is to define such projections solely in terms of manifest predicates.

Everyone knows, we are often told, that a thing not under pressure is called flexible if it is of the same kind as the things that flex; or in other words, that if among things under suitable pressure, "flexes" applies to all and only those that are of kind K, then "flexible" applies to all and only things that are of kind K whether they are under pressure or not. Nothing could be much simpler—or much less illuminating. For just when are two things of the same kind? Merely to belong to some one class is not enough; for *any* two things belong to some one class. And to belong to all the same classes is far too much; for no two things belong to all the same classes. Perhaps, then, to be of the same kind is to have the same 'essential' properties? I shall spare you a diatribe on the notion of essentiality, and remark only that even should we take the distinction between essential and accidental for granted, it might not help much in the present context. For whereas our problem is to give an explanation in terms of manifest predicates, we might well find that only dispositional predicates are essential and all manifest predicates accidental.[9]

What matters is not how essential a property is but how it is related to the manifest property we start from. If certain other manifest properties are somehow intimately connected with flexing, not merely casual accompaniments of it, exhibition of these properties by a thing not under pressure will be grounds for regarding the thing as flexible. In other words, we can define "flexible" if we find an auxiliary manifest predicate that is suitably related to "flexes" through 'causal' principles or *laws*. The problem of dispositions is to define the nature of the connection involved here: the problem of characterizing a relation such that if the initial manifest predicate "Q" stands in this relation to another manifest predicate or conjunction of manifest predicates "A", then "A" may be equated with the dispositional counterpart—"Q-able" or "Q$_D$"—of the predicate "Q". But the question when such a 'causal' connection obtains or how laws are to be dis-

---

[9] For the essential characters of things are usually thought of as enduring, and it is the predicates for enduring characters that we normally regard as dispositional. Thus those who propose to deal with the problem of dispositions by means of classes defined in terms of the microcosmic structure of things often beg the question; for among the dispositional predicates they set out to explain lie the very predicates they need for describing these structures.

tinguished from accidental truths is an especially perplexing one.

In this grim picture, we can find one small note of comfort. Observe first that solution of the general problem will not automatically provide us with a definition for each dispositional predicate; we shall need additional special knowledge in order to find the auxiliary predicate that satisfies the general formula—i.e. that is related in the requisite way to the initial manifest predicate. But on the other hand, discovery of a suitable definition for a given dispositional predicate need not in all cases wait upon solution of the general problem. If luck or abundant special information turns up a manifest predicate "P" that we are confident coincides in its application with "flexible", we can use "P" as definiens for "flexible" without inquiring further about the nature of its connection with "flexes". This point needs to be borne in mind because in any investigation, even the present one, we may on occasion find that important progress can be made if one particular dispositional predicate can be defined. In that case, lack of a general formula ought not to deter us from a real try at defining the predicate in question.

Some, of course, object that the effort to define ordinary physical disposition-terms is philosophically immoral.[10] The scientist, it is held, never defines such a term;

---

[10] The view to be discussed in this and the following paragraph is by now so prevalent that I felt it must be dealt with here even at the cost of digressing from the main course of our investigation. See Carnap, 'Testability and Meaning' in *Philosophy of Science*, vol. 3 (1936), especially p. 449; Kaplan, 'Definition and Specification of Meaning' in the *Journal of Philosophy*, vol. xliii (1946), pp. 281-8—also my review of this article in the *Journal of Sym-*

he partially and progressively specifies its meaning as he learns more and more. To represent scientific procedure accurately, then, we ought to introduce these terms as primitives, by means of postulates, and add new postulates as needed.[11] This does not bear on what I have called the general problem of dispositions but on the question of defining specific disposition-terms; yet even here the point seems to me ill-taken. Philosophy, to my way of thinking, has rather the function of explicating scientific—and everyday—language than of depicting scientific or everyday procedure. While explication must respect the presystematic application of terms, it need not reflect the manner or order of their presystematic adoption; rather it must seek maximum coherence and articulation. Thus a legitimate and sufficient incentive for introducing terms into the explanatory discourse by means of definition wherever possible, rather than as primitives, lies in the economy and resultant integration thereby achieved. The

---

bolic Logic, vol. 11 (1946), p. 80; and Hempel, *Fundamentals of Concept Formation*, Chicago, 1952, pp. 28-9.

[11] There are just two ways of introducing terms into a system: (1) as primitives, (2) by definition. Passages in the Carnap article cited in Note 10 have given rise to the impression that there is a new, third, method of introducing terms: by reduction sentences. Carnap writes, for example, (p. 443): "If we wish to construct a language for science we have to take some descriptive (i.e. nonlogical) terms as primitive terms. Further terms may then be introduced not only by explicit definitions but also by other reduction sentences. The possibility of introduction . . . by physical reduction is very important for science but so far not sufficiently noted in the logical analysis of science." This is rather misleading; for to introduce a term by means of reduction postulates is to introduce it as an ineliminable primitive.

argument that we do better to refrain from defining a term in explanatory discourse unless that term is customarily defined by scientists or laymen is like the argument that philosophy ought not to be coherent unless the reality it describes is coherent. One might as well argue that philosophy should not be written in English because the world is not written in English. There is no positive virtue in not defining disposition terms.

Still, it is sometimes contended that to define even the most ordinary dispositional predicates is so inordinately difficult that if we refuse to use other means than definition for introducing them into our system, we shall be forced either to forego introducing them altogether or else to use tentative definitions that will soon have to be withdrawn. This overlooks the fact that wherever we are prepared to set up reduction postulates for given dispositional predicates, we have the alternative of setting up definitions for more restricted dispositional predicates. If, for example, we decide that exhibition of a given spectroscopic pattern is a good sign of the flexibility of a thing and yet want to leave the way open for other tests that may prove useful when neither suitable pressure nor spectroscopic inspection can be applied, we may define the predicate "flexible-thing-under-pressure-or-spectroscopic-inspection" and the predicate "inflexible-thing-under-pressure-or-spectroscopic-inspection".[12] This defi-

_____

[12] The first of these hyphenated predicates will be defined as applying to all and only those things that either are under suitable pressure and bend, or are spectroscopically inspected and exhibit the pattern in question. The second hyphenated predicate will be defined as applying to all and only those things that either are under suitable pressure and fail to bend, or are spectroscopically inspected and fail to exhibit the pattern in question. (These for-

nitionally projects the "flex"–"fails to flex" dichotomy to a wider though not universal realm, and has the advantage that the predicates introduced are fully eliminable.

However, nothing in this digression on the desirability of defining dispositional predicates helps to solve the central and pressing problem of the nature of the relation between initial manifest predicates and the manifest predicates used to project them. This general problem of dispositions remains independent of the decision whether such auxiliaries when found are to be employed in definitions or in reduction postulates.

In closing this brief survey of the problem of dispositions, I suggest that two points be kept in mind for future reference: the formulation of the general problem, and the recognition that dispositional as well as manifest predicates are labels used in classifying *actual* things.

4. Possibles

While dispositional statements may be treated as speaking of actual things, what of other statements that ostensibly speak of possible entities?

Let us begin with a case rather far removed from the context of our preceding discussion. Suppose we are using not a physicalistic thing-language but a phenomenalistic language for which the atomic elements are places in the visual field, moments of phenomenal time, minimal phenomenal colors, sounds, etc.[13] Now there are moments —for example, when one eye is closed—when the visual

---

mulations, like earlier passages in the above text, have been simplified by using "things" not for long-enduring objects but for brief temporal segments of them.)

[13] Such a system is outlined in *The Structure of Appearance*, cited in Note 2; see especially Chapter VI.

field is smaller (that is, contains fewer phenomenal places) than at other moments. Select a certain moment t at which the field is thus narrowed, and a certain place p that is not presented at the moment t. Both p and t are actual phenomenal elements,[14] but there is no such entity as the place-time composed of p and t. Nevertheless, we must often talk about this fictive place-time. The question of its (possible) color, for example, is regarded as legitimate and may be important to knowledge.

We have here a very simple example of the filling in of gaps in actual experience with a fabric of possibles. The problem of what to do about such fictive or possible sense-data inevitably confronts the phenomenalist at an early stage in his work. I am afraid that too often he resigns himself to letting possible sense-data in on the ground floor along with actual sense-data. While he may succeed in teaching himself to do this without choking or blushing, his critics happily chalk up a fatal concession.

To return to our example, the situation is this: there is no such place-time as place-p-at-time-t, and every statement affirming that some color occurs at this place-time is false. How then, without introducing the fictive place-time as an element, can we frame the question we want to ask about the color at this place-time? We may, of course, put the question in counterfactual form; but we have seen that there is little help in that direction.

---

[14] This statement is of course to be taken as tenseless. Tenselessly speaking, a place or color that occurs at any time is actual, just as Thales is an actual man. An actual color or place need not occur at all times any more than an actual man need live forever. See *The Structure of Appearance*, Chapter VI, Section 4; Chapter XI.

The first thing to observe in our example is that although there is no such *place-time* as p-at-t, there *is* the actual entity comprised of p and t, whether we choose to treat it as the class $\{p, t\}$ or—as I shall here—as the sum individual $p + t$.[15] This entity, for lack of a certain relationship among its parts, misses being a place-time much as the scattered whole comprised of the body of one automobile and the chassis of another across the street misses being an automobile. In other words, the predicate "place-time", though it applies to many entities composed of a place and a time, does not apply to others, such as our $p + t$. To speak of the "fictive" or "possible" place-time $p + t$ is not to speak of a new non-actual entity but to say something new about (i.e. apply a new predicate to) the old actual entity $p + t$. For some purposes we want to consider together under one heading all place-times and certain other entities like $p + t$. The usual heading is such a predicate as "possible place-time". The class of possible place-times is, then, simply a certain class of actual entities that includes the smaller class of actual place-times.

The relation between the predicates "place-time" and "possible place-time" is thus closely analogous to that between "flexes" and "flexible"; indeed, only grammatical primness prevents us from describing $p + t$ as 'place-time-able' rather than as a 'possible place-time'. Of course, as

---

[15] The sign "$+$" as used here belongs to the calculus of individuals and "$p + t$" simply stands for the whole comprised of p and t. The reader who wants fuller explanation may consult Chapter II, Section 4, of *The Structure of Appearance*, while the reader who shudders at the thought of adding individuals may sustitute "$\{p, t\}$"—standing for the class having p and t as members—throughout our present discussion.

with disposition-terms, our way of putting the matter shifts the burden to the question how the projection is made. In the present example, the projection happens to be easy; for "possible place-time" may well be defined as applying to all and only those entities that are made up of one place and one time. But we may on occasion use the same predicate to cover a class that is wider or narrower than this and harder to define. And other questions, such as our question about what color occurs at $p + t$ (or, as we may now frame it, the question which color predicate is to be projected over $p + t$) may raise subtle and difficult problems of projection. Nevertheless, a way of reinterpreting some ostensible references to other than actual sense-data has at least been outlined.

To repeat the main point, if $p + t$ is not a place-time and so has no color occurring at it, the predicate "place-time" obviously applies only to certain other wholes consisting of a place and a time, and the predicate "crimson" (i.e. "crimson occurs at") applies only to some among these place-times. The elliptical statement that the place-time $p + t$ is crimson is then to be interpreted as involving two projections. It projects both the predicate "place-time" and the predicate "crimson" over the actual entity $p + t$; or better, it applies to $p + t$ a certain projection of "place-time" and a certain projection of "crimson".

Yet how are we to deal with a case where, so to speak, instead of thus filling in gaps, we are describing alternatives to actual experiences? Suppose, for example, that at a certain actual place-time $p_1 + t_1$, the color emerald green actually occurs; but suppose that (because, say, I was looking at a wall painted in blue and green stripes) the color cobalt blue 'would have occurred' at the visual place p_1 at the time t_1, had my head been turned further to the right at the time. Consider now the ascription to this place-time, $p_1 + t_1$, of the color cobalt blue under the hypothetical circumstance (call it circumstance "C") that my head was turned slightly further to the right than it actually was. This problem looks different from our first one because we have here no entities like our old $p + t$ waiting around to be assigned colors; the actual place-time $p_1 + t_1$ already has one color, and it cannot have two. Rather than patching in our actual experience, we seem here to be starting to portray a whole new possible experience. Even so, this case can be handled in much the same way. To say that $p_1 + t_1$ is actually green but is possibly (i.e. under circumstance C) blue is in effect to ascribe to $p_1 + t_1$, in addition to the predicate "green", some such predicate as "C-blueable".[16] This predicate, again, simply projects the predicate "blue" over a certain wider range of actual entities. And just as "C-blueable" may apply to the same place-time that "green" does, so may other predicates as well; for example, where D, E,

---

[16] "C-blueable" and a predicate such as "E-blueable"—applying to place-times that are blue under the different circumstance E— are related much as "water soluble" and "acid soluble". Incidentally, I trust it will be understood that I do not advocate daily use of barbarous predicates like "place-timeable" and "C-blueable" but introduce them solely for expository purposes. In daily discourse, we usually make familiar predicates like "blue" and "possibly blue" serve many different purposes in different contexts. We often apply "blue" not only to things that are actually blue but also to things that are blue under some particularly important fictive circumstance; and we use "possibly blue" for things that are blue under whatever fictive circumstance is explicitly or implicitly indicated by the context.

and F are other circumstances, all the predicates "D-red-able", "E-blueable", and "F-whiteable" may also apply to $p_1 + t_1$.

Leaving the language of phenomenalism, let us now look at statements concerning possible physical events. From what has been said already it is clear how to proceed. For when we say that a certain thing k is flexible at time s, we are in effect describing a fictive event happening to k at s. The actual event that is the temporal segment of k that occupies s is not a flexing event; but to speak of it as a possible flexing event is simply to classify it under the dispositional predicate "flexible". Familiar dispositional predicates are not always available; but once the principle is understood, new predicates can be coined as needed. The fictive accident to a given train under the hypothetical circumstance that a given rail was missing can be taken care of, for example, by saying that the train at that time was "accidentable" or, more fully, "rail-missing-accident-able".

Perhaps I should remind you that I am discussing just those possible occurrences that we know to be non-actual. If a train is late and I say that it possibly had an accident, I am saying no more than that I do not know that it has not had an accident. But if I know that the train has arrived after a normal run, any talk of possible accidents to it on the way must obviously have a quite different interpretation. The difference is the difference between saying that a train may have had an accident (when I don't know whether it had one or not) and saying that a train might have had an accident (when I know that it had none). Statements of the latter sort present the more acute problem of translation, and it is these alone that I am concerned with here.

Offhand, we might expect to encounter new difficulties when faced with discourse ostensibly pertaining to non-actual enduring things rather than to non-actual happenings to actual things; but even such discourse can readily be interpreted as the application of certain predicates to certain actual things. We can truthfully put fictive mountains in the middle of London simply by applying to London a certain projection of the predicate "mountainous".[17]

I am not at all attempting, of course, to provide means for determining the truth or falsity of statements about possibles, but suggesting a way of translating these statements into statements about actuals. Once such a translation has been accomplished, the question of determining the truth or falsity of the statement is simply a question of ascertaining a matter of fact.

Thus we begin to perceive the general way in which statements affirming that certain possible so-and-sos are not actual so-and-sos may be reconciled with the doctrine that the only possible entities are actual ones. To consider further special cases would be to risk losing ourselves in a

---

[17] Although we talk in general of possibles, we are seldom concerned with what is merely possible, i.e. possible under some stateable circumstance or other. We are more often concerned with what occurs under some specific fictive circumstance. Thus the mountains we are likely to put in London are not merely-possible mountains, but mountains that belong there under, for example, the fictive circumstance that a certain volcanic action took place.

welter of detail. It should merely be remarked that some 'predicates of possibles' may not be simple projections of manifest predicates but may extensionally intersect them in more complicated ways.[18] However, the question naturally arises whether, if we restrict ourselves to predicates of actual things, we shall have enough equipment to say about the actual everything we need to say that ordinarily passes for talk about the possible. It is comforting to observe that if there are only three atomic elements, then there are seven individuals in all, and these supply differing extensions (none of them null) for some 127 one-place predicates. For any normal system that admits at least hundreds of atomic elements, either phenomenal or physical, the number of available extensions runs into billions. The threat of enforced silence is remote.

My main purpose here, then, has been to suggest that discourse, even about possibles, need not transgress the

---

[18] The predicate "flexible" is a simple projection of the predicate "flexes"; for all things that flex and some that do not flex are flexible. But I use the term "projection" broadly enough to count "flexible" as a projection of "bends" also, even though some things that bend (e.g. under extraordinary pressure) are not flexible. Again, the dispositional predicate "is orange" is a projection of the manifest predicate "looks orange", even though not everything that looks orange (e.g. under yellow light) is orange. In these examples, "projection" in effect covers two steps: the elimination of certain cases belonging to the extension of the original manifest predicate (e.g. the step from "bends" to "flexes", or from "looks orange" to "looks orange in daylight"); and the addition of other cases, not belonging to the extension of the narrower manifest predicate thus arrived at (e.g. the step from "flexes" to "flexible", or from "looks orange in daylight" to "is orange").

boundaries of the actual world. What we often mistake for the actual world is one particular description of it. And what we mistake for possible worlds are just equally true descriptions in other terms. We have come to think of the actual as one among many possible worlds. We need to repaint that picture. All possible worlds lie within the actual one.

5. *The Passing*

Possible processes and possible entities vanish. Predicates supposedly pertaining to them are seen to apply to actual things, but to have extensions related in peculiar ways to, and usually broader than, the extensions of certain manifest predicates. A predicate ostensibly of possibles as compared to a correlative manifest predicate, like an open umbrella as compared to a closed one, simply covers more of the same earthly stuff.

Our attention is thus centered upon what I have called the general problem of dispositions, which has in effect become the general problem of possibles as well. To repeat, this is the problem of explaining how a given manifest predicate, say "P", must be related to others if the fact that these others apply to a thing is to be ground for applying to that thing a broader correlative of "P"—say "Pj". I have spoken of this as a problem of projection because it is the problem how, beginning with a manifest predicate like "burns", we can in effect spread it over a wider range by defining a correlative predicate like "inflammable" that covers things that burn and certain other things also, but nothing that *fails* to burn.

Now the problem of making the projection from manifest to non-manifest cases is obviously not very different from the problem of going from known to unknown or from past to future cases. The problem of dispositions looks suspiciously like one of the philosopher's oldest friends and enemies: the problem of induction. Indeed, the two are but different aspects of the general problem of proceeding from a given set of cases to a wider set. The critical questions throughout are the same: when, how, why is such a transition or expansion legitimate? In the next lecture, then, we must see how matters stand at present with the familiar problem of induction.

Thus passes the possible. It passes, indeed, only into another and exceedingly difficult problem. But that problem has been troubling our sleep for a long time on its own account. There is perhaps some solace in the thought that at least the ghost of the possible will no longer be thumping in the attic.

III

THE NEW RIDDLE OF INDUCTION

1. The Old Problem of Induction

At the close of the preceding lecture, I said that today I should examine how matters stand with respect to the problem of induction. In a word, I think they stand ill. But the real difficulties that confront us today are not the traditional ones. What is commonly thought of as the Problem of Induction has been solved, or dissolved; and we face new problems that are not as yet very widely understood. To approach them, I shall have to run as quickly as possible over some very familiar ground.

The problem of the validity of judgments about future or unknown cases arises, as Hume pointed out, because such judgments are neither reports of experience nor logical consequences of it. Predictions, of course, pertain to what has not yet been observed. And they cannot be logically inferred from what has been observed; for what *has* happened imposes no logical restrictions on what *will* happen. Although Hume's dictum that there are no necessary connections of matters of fact has been challenged at times, it has withstood all attacks. Indeed, I should be inclined not merely to agree that there are no necessary connections of matters of fact, but to ask whether there are any necessary connections at all[1]—but that is another story.

Hume's answer to the question how predictions are related to past experience is refreshingly non-cosmic. When an event of one kind frequently follows upon an event of another kind in experience, a habit is formed that leads the mind, when confronted with a new event of the first kind, to pass to the idea of an event of the second kind. The idea of necessary connection arises from the felt impulse of the mind in making this transition.

Now if we strip this account of all extraneous features, the central point is that to the question "Why one prediction rather than another?", Hume answers that the elect prediction is one that accords with a past regularity, because this regularity has established a habit. Thus among alternative statements about a future moment, one statement is distinguished by its consonance with habit and thus with regularities observed in the past. Prediction according to any other alternative is errant.

How satisfactory is this answer? The heaviest criticism has taken the righteous position that Hume's account at best pertains only to the source of predictions, not their legitimacy; that he sets forth the circumstances under which we make given predictions—and in this sense explains why we make them—but leaves untouched the

---

[1] Although this remark is merely an aside, perhaps I should explain for the sake of some unusually sheltered reader that the notion of a necessary connection of ideas, or of an absolutely analytic statement, is no longer sacrosanct. Some, like Quine and White, have forthrightly attacked the notion; others, like myself, have simply discarded it; and still others have begun to feel acutely uncomfortable about it.

question of our license for making them. To trace origins, runs the old complaint, is not to establish validity: the real question is not why a prediction is in fact made but how it can be justified. Since this seems to point to the awkward conclusion that the greatest of modern philosophers completely missed the point of his own problem, the idea has developed that he did not really take his solution very seriously, but regarded the main problem as unsolved and perhaps as insoluble. Thus we come to speak of 'Hume's problem' as though he propounded it as a question without answer.

All this seems to me quite wrong. I think Hume grasped the central question and considered his answer to be passably effective. And I think his answer is reasonable and relevant, even if it is not entirely satisfactory. I shall explain presently. At the moment, I merely want to record a protest against the prevalent notion that the problem of justifying induction, when it is so sharply dissociated from the problem of describing how induction takes place, can fairly be called Hume's problem.

I suppose that the problem of justifying induction has called forth as much fruitless discussion as has any halfway respectable problem of modern philosophy. The typical writer begins by insisting that some way of justifying predictions must be found; proceeds to argue that for this purpose we need some resounding universal law of the Uniformity of Nature, and then inquires how this universal principle itself can be justified. At this point, if he is tired, he concludes that the principle must be accepted as an indispensable assumption; or if he is energetic and ingenious, he goes on to devise some subtle justification for it. Such an invention, however, seldom satisfies anyone else; and the easier course of accepting an unsubstantiated and even dubious assumption much more sweeping than any actual predictions we make seems an odd and expensive way of justifying them.

2. Dissolution of the Old Problem

Understandably, then, more critical thinkers have suspected that there might be something awry with the problem we are trying to solve. Come to think of it, what precisely would constitute the justification we seek? If the problem is to explain how we know that certain predictions will turn out to be correct, the sufficient answer is that we don't know any such thing. If the problem is to *find* some way of distinguishing antecedently between true and false predictions, we are asking for prevision rather than for philosophical explanation. Nor does it help matters much to say that we are merely trying to show that or why certain predictions are *probable*. Often it is said that while we cannot tell in advance whether a prediction concerning a given throw of a die is true, we can decide whether the prediction is a probable one. But if this means determining how the prediction is related to actual frequency distributions of future throws of the die, surely there is no way of knowing or proving this in advance. On the other hand, if the judgment that the prediction is probable has nothing to do with subsequent occurrences, then the question remains in what sense a probable prediction is any better justified than an improbable one.

Now obviously the genuine problem cannot be one of attaining unattainable knowledge or of accounting for knowledge that we do not in fact have. A better understanding of our problem can be gained by looking for a moment at what is involved in justifying non-inductive inferences. How do we justify a *de*duction? Plainly, by showing that it conforms to the general rules of deductive inference. An argument that so conforms is justified or valid, even if its conclusion happens to be false. An argument that violates a rule is fallacious even if its conclusion happens to be true. To justify a deductive conclusion therefore requires no knowledge of the facts it pertains to. Moreover, when a deductive argument has been shown to conform to the rules of logical inference, we usually consider it justified without going on to ask what justifies the rules. Analogously, the basic task in justifying an inductive inference is to show that it conforms to the general rules of *in*duction. Once we have recognized this, we have gone a long way towards clarifying our problem.

Yet, of course, the rules themselves must eventually be justified. The validity of a deduction depends not upon conformity to any purely arbitrary rules we may contrive, but upon conformity to valid rules. When we speak of *the* rules of inference we mean the valid rules—or better, *some* valid rules, since there may be alternative sets of equally valid rules. But how is the validity of rules to be determined? Here again we encounter philosophers who insist that these rules follow from some self-evident axiom, and others who try to show that the rules are grounded in the very nature of the human mind. I think the answer lies much nearer the surface. Principles of deductive inference are justified by their conformity with accepted deductive practice. Their validity depends upon accordance with the particular deductive inferences we actually make and sanction. If a rule yields inacceptable inferences, we drop it as invalid. Justification of general rules thus derives from judgments rejecting or accepting particular deductive inferences.

This looks flagrantly circular. I have said that deductive inferences are justified by their conformity to valid general rules, and that general rules are justified by their conformity to valid inferences. But this circle is a virtuous one. The point is that rules and particular inferences alike are justified by being brought into agreement with each other. *A rule is amended if it yields an inference we are unwilling to accept; an inference is rejected if it violates a rule we are unwilling to amend.* The process of justification is the delicate one of making mutual adjustments between rules and accepted inferences; and in the agreement achieved lies the only justification needed for either.

All this applies equally well to induction. An inductive inference, too, is justified by conformity to general rules, and a general rule by conformity to accepted inductive inferences. Predictions are justified if they conform to valid canons of induction; and the canons are valid if they accurately codify accepted inductive practice.

A result of such analysis is that we can stop plaguing ourselves with certain spurious questions about induction. We no longer demand an explanation for guarantees that we do not have, or seek keys to knowledge that we cannot obtain. It dawns upon us that the traditional smug insistence upon a hard-and-fast line between justifying induction and describing ordinary inductive practice distorts the problem. And we owe belated apologies to Hume. For in dealing with the question how normally accepted inductive judgments are made, he was in fact dealing with the question of inductive validity.[2] The validity of a prediction consisted for him in its arising from habit, and thus in its exemplifying some past regularity. His answer was incomplete and perhaps not entirely correct; but it was not beside the point. The problem of induction is not a problem of demonstration but a problem of defining the difference between valid and invalid predictions.

This clears the air but leaves a lot to be done. As principles of *de*ductive inference, we have the familiar and highly developed laws of logic; but there are available no such precisely stated and well-recognized principles of inductive inference. Mill's canons hardly rank with Aristotle's rules of the syllogism, let alone with *Principia*

---

[2] A hasty reader might suppose that my insistence here upon identifying the problem of justification with a problem of description is out of keeping with my parenthetical insistence in the preceding lecture that the goal of philosophy is something quite different from the mere description of ordinary or scientific procedure. Let me repeat that the point urged there was that the organization of the explanatory account need not reflect the manner or order in which predicates are adopted in practice. It surely must describe practice, however, in the sense that the extensions of predicates as explicated must conform in certain ways to the extensions of the same predicates as applied in practice. Hume's account is a description in just this sense. For it is an attempt to set forth the circumstances under which those inductive judgments are made that are normally accepted as valid; and to do that is to state necessary and sufficient conditions for, and thus to define, valid induction. What I am maintaining above is that the problem of justifying induction is not something over and above the problem of describing or defining valid induction.

Mathematica. Elaborate and valuable treatises on probability usually leave certain fundamental questions untouched. Only in very recent years has there been any explicit and systematic work upon what I call the constructive task of confirmation theory.

3. *The Constructive Task of Confirmation Theory*

The task of formulating rules that define the difference between valid and invalid inductive inferences is much like the task of defining any term with an established usage. If we set out to define the term "tree", we try to compose out of already understood words an expression that will apply to the familiar objects that standard usage calls trees, and that will not apply to objects that standard usage refuses to call trees. A proposal that plainly violates either condition is rejected; while a definition that meets these tests may be adopted and used to decide cases that are not already settled by actual usage. Thus the interplay we observed between rules of induction and particular inductive inferences is simply an instance of this characteristic dual adjustment between definition and usage, whereby the usage informs the definition, which in turn guides extension of the usage.

Of course this adjustment is a more complex matter than I have indicated. Sometimes, in the interest of convenience or theoretical utility, we deliberately permit a definition to run counter to clear mandates of common usage. We accept a definition of "fish" that excludes whales. Similarly we may decide to deny the term "valid induction" to some inductive inferences that are commonly considered valid, or apply the term to others not usually so considered. A definition may modify as well as extend ordinary usage.[3]

Some pioneer work on the problem of defining confirmation or valid induction has been done by Professor Hempel.[4] Let me remind you briefly of a few of his results. Just as deductive logic is concerned primarily with a relation between statements—namely the consequence relation—that is independent of their truth or falsity, so inductive logic as Hempel conceives it is concerned primarily with a comparable relation of confirmation between statements. Thus the problem is to define the relation that obtains between any statement S_1 and another S_2 if and only if S_1 may properly be said to confirm S_2 in any degree.

With the question so stated, the first step seems obvious. Does not induction proceed in just the opposite direction from deduction? Surely some of the evidence-statements that inductively support a general hypothesis are consequences of it. Since the consequence relation is already well defined by deductive logic, will we not be on firm ground in saying that confirmation embraces the converse relation? The laws of deduction in reverse will then be among the laws of induction.

Let's see where this leads us. We naturally assume fur-

---

[3] For a fuller discussion of definition in general see Chapter I of *The Structure of Appearance*.

[4] The basic article is 'A Purely Syntactical Definition of Confirmation', cited in Note I.10. A much less technical account is given in 'Studies in the Logic of Confirmation', *Mind*, n.s., vol. 54 (1945), pp. 1–26 and 97–121. Later work by Hempel and others on defining *degree* of confirmation does not concern us here.

ther that whatever confirms a given statement confirms also whatever follows from that statement.[5] But if we combine this assumption with our proposed principle, we get the embarrassing result that every statement confirms every other. Surprising as it may be that such innocent beginnings lead to such an intolerable conclusion, the proof is very easy. Start with any statement S_1. It is a consequence of, and so by our present criterion confirms, the conjunction of S_1 and any statement whatsoever—call it S_2. But the confirmed conjunction, $S_1 \cdot S_2$, of course has S_2 as a consequence. Thus every statement confirms all statements.

The fault lies in careless formulation of our first proposal. While some statements that confirm a general hypothesis are consequences of it, not all its consequences confirm it. This may not be immediately evident; for indeed we do in some sense furnish support for a statement when we establish one of its consequences. We settle one of the questions about it. Consider the heterogeneous conjunction:

---

[5] I am not here asserting that this is an indispensable requirement upon a definition of confirmation. Since our commonsense assumptions taken in combination quickly lead us to absurd conclusions, some of these assumptions have to be dropped; and different theorists may make different decisions about which to drop and which to preserve. Hempel gives up the converse consequence condition, while Carnap (*Logical Foundations of Probability*, Chicago and London, 1950, pp. 474–6) drops both the consequence condition and the converse consequence condition. Such differences of detail between different treatments of confirmation do not affect the central points I am making in this lecture.

8497 is a prime number and the other side of the moon is flat and Elizabeth the First was crowned on a Tuesday.

To show that any one of the three component statements is true is to support the conjunction by reducing the net undetermined claim. But support[6] of this kind is not confirmation; for establishment of one component endows the whole statement with no credibility that is transmitted to other component statements. Confirmation of a hypothesis occurs only when an instance imparts to the hypothesis some credibility that is conveyed to other instances. Appraisal of hypotheses, indeed, is incidental to prediction, to the judgment of new cases on the basis of old ones.

Our formula thus needs tightening. This is readily accomplished, as Hempel points out, if we observe that a hypothesis is genuinely confirmed only by a statement that is an instance of it in the special sense of entailing not the hypothesis itself but its relativization or restriction to the class of entities mentioned by that statement. The relativization of a general hypothesis to a class results from restricting the range of its universal and existential quantifiers to the members of that class. Less technically, what the hypothesis says of all things the evidence statement says of one thing (or

---

[6] Any hypothesis is 'supported' by its own positive instances; but support—or better, direct factual support—is only one factor in confirmation. This factor has been separately studied by John G. Kemeny and Paul Oppenheim in 'Degree of Factual Support', *Philosophy of Science*, vol. 19 (1952), pp. 307–24. As will appear presently, my concern in these lectures is primarily with certain other important factors in confirmation, some of them quite generally neglected.

of one pair or other n-ad of things). This obviously covers the confirmation of the conductivity of all copper by the conductivity of a given piece; and it excludes confirmation of our heterogeneous conjunction by any of its components. And, when taken together with the principle that what confirms a statement confirms all its consequences, this criterion does not yield the untoward conclusion that every statement confirms every other.

New difficulties promptly appear from other directions, however. One is the infamous paradox of the ravens. The statement that a given object, say this piece of paper, is neither black nor a raven confirms the hypothesis that all non-black things are non-ravens. But this hypothesis is logically equivalent to the hypothesis that all ravens are black. Hence we arrive at the unexpected conclusion that the statement that a given object is neither black nor a raven confirms the hypothesis that all ravens are black. The prospect of being able to investigate ornithological theories without going out in the rain is so attractive that we know there must be a catch in it. The trouble this time, however, lies not in faulty definition, but in tacit and illicit reference to evidence not stated in our example. Taken by itself, the statement that the given object is neither black nor a raven confirms the hypothesis that everything that is not a raven is not black as well as the hypothesis that everything that is not black is not a raven. We tend to ignore the former hypothesis because we know it to be false from abundant other evidence—from all the familiar things that are not ravens but are black. But we are required to assume that no such evidence is available. Under this circumstance, even a much stronger hypothesis is also obviously confirmed: that nothing is either black or a raven. In the light of this confirmation of the hypothesis that there are no ravens, it is no longer surprising that under the artificial restrictions of the example, the hypothesis that all ravens are black is also confirmed. And the prospects for indoor ornithology vanish when we notice that under these same conditions, the contrary hypothesis that no ravens are black is equally well confirmed.[7]

On the other hand, our definition does err in not forcing us to take into account all the *stated* evidence. The unhappy results are readily illustrated. If two compatible evidence statements confirm two hypotheses, then naturally the conjunction of the evidence statements should confirm the conjunction of the hypotheses.[8] Suppose our evidence consists of the statements E_1 saying that a given thing b is black, and E_2 saying that a second thing c is not black. By our present definition, E_1 confirms the hypothesis that everything is black, and E_2 the hypothesis that everything is non-black. The conjunction of these perfectly compatible evidence statements will then confirm the self-contradictory hypothesis that everything is both black and non-black. Simple as this anomaly is, it requires drastic modification of our definition. What given evidence confirms

---

[7] An able and thorough exposition of this paragraph is given by Israel Scheffler in his *Anatomy of Inquiry*, New York, 1963, pp. 286–91.

[8] The status of the conjunction condition is much like that of the consequence condition—see Note III.5. Although Carnap drops the conjunction condition also (p. 394), he adopts for different reasons the requirement we find needed above: that the total available evidence must always be taken into account (pp. 211–13).

is not what we arrive at by generalizing from separate items of it, but—roughly speaking—what we arrive at by generalizing from the total stated evidence. The central idea for an improved definition is that, within certain limitations, what is asserted to be true for the narrow universe of the evidence statements is confirmed for the whole universe of discourse. Thus if our evidence is E_1 and E_2, neither the hypothesis that all things are black nor the hypothesis that all things are non-black is confirmed; for neither is true for the evidence-universe consisting of b and c. Of course, much more careful formulation is needed, since some statements that are true of the evidence-universe—such as that there is only one black thing—are obviously not confirmed for the whole universe. These matters are taken care of by the studied formal definition that Hempel develops on this basis; but we cannot and need not go into further detail here.

No one supposes that the task of confirmation-theory has been completed. But the few steps I have reviewed—chosen partly for their bearing on what is to follow—show how things move along once the problem of definition displaces the problem of justification. Important and long-unnoticed questions are brought to light and answered; and we are encouraged to expect that the many remaining questions will in time yield to similar treatment.

But our satisfaction is shortlived. New and serious trouble begins to appear.

4. The New Riddle of Induction

Confirmation of a hypothesis by an instance depends rather heavily upon features of the hypothesis other than its syntactical form. That a given piece of copper conducts electricity increases the credibility of statements asserting that other pieces of copper conduct electricity, and thus confirms the hypothesis that all copper conducts electricity. But the fact that a given man now in this room is a third son does not increase the credibility of statements asserting that other men now in this room are third sons, and so does not confirm the hypothesis that all men now in this room are third sons. Yet in both cases our hypothesis is a generalization of the evidence statement. The difference is that in the former case the hypothesis is a *lawlike* statement; while in the latter case, the hypothesis is a merely contingent or accidental generality. Only a statement that is *lawlike*—regardless of its truth or falsity or its scientific importance—is capable of receiving confirmation from an instance of it; accidental statements are not. Plainly, then, we must look for a way of distinguishing lawlike from accidental statements.

So long as what seems to be needed is merely a way of excluding a few odd and unwanted cases that are inadvertently admitted by our definition of confirmation, the problem may not seem very hard or very pressing. We fully expect that minor defects will be found in our definition and that the necessary refinements will have to be worked out patiently one after another. But some further examples will show that our present difficulty is of a much graver kind.

Suppose that all emeralds examined before a certain time *t* are green.[9] At time *t*, then, our observations support the

---

[9] Although the example used is different, the argument to follow is substantially the same as that set forth in my note 'A Query on Confirmation', cited in Note I.16.

hypothesis that all emeralds are green; and this is in accord with our definition of confirmation. Our evidence statements assert that emerald a is green, that emerald b is green, and so on; and each confirms the general hypothesis that all emeralds are green. So far, so good.

Now let me introduce another predicate less familiar than "green". It is the predicate "grue" and it applies to all things examined before t just in case they are green but to other things just in case they are blue. Then at time t we have, for each evidence statement asserting that a given emerald is green, a parallel evidence statement asserting that that emerald is grue. And the statements that emerald a is grue, that emerald b is grue, and so on, will each confirm the general hypothesis that all emeralds are grue. Thus according to our definition, the prediction that all emeralds subsequently examined will be green and the prediction that all will be grue are alike confirmed by evidence statements describing the same observations. But if an emerald subsequently examined is grue, it is blue and hence not green. Thus although we are well aware which of the two incompatible predictions is genuinely confirmed, they are equally well confirmed according to our present definition. Moreover, it is clear that if we simply choose an appropriate predicate, then on the basis of these same observations we shall have equal confirmation, by our definition, for any prediction whatever about other emeralds—or indeed about anything else.[10] As in our earlier example, only the predictions subsumed under law-

---

[10] For instance, we shall have equal confirmation, by our present definition, for the prediction that roses subsequently examined will be blue. Let "emerose" apply just to emeralds examined before time t, and to roses examined later. Then all emeroses so far examined are grue, and this confirms the hypothesis that all

like hypotheses are genuinely confirmed; but we have no criterion as yet for determining lawlikeness. And now we see that without some such criterion, our definition not merely includes a few unwanted cases, but is so completely ineffectual that it virtually excludes nothing. We are left once again with the intolerable result that anything confirms anything. This difficulty cannot be set aside as an annoying detail to be taken care of in due course. It has to be met before our definition will work at all.

Nevertheless, the difficulty is often slighted because on the surface there seem to be easy ways of dealing with it. Sometimes, for example, the problem is thought to be much like the paradox of the ravens. We are here again, it is pointed out, making tacit and illegitimate use of information outside the stated evidence: the information, for example, that different samples of one material are usually alike in conductivity, and the information that different men in a lecture audience are usually not alike in the number of their older brothers. But while it is true that such information is being smuggled in, this does not by itself settle the matter as it settles the matter of the ravens. There the point was that when the smuggled information is forthrightly declared, its effect upon the confirmation of the hypothesis in question is immediately and properly registered by the definition we are using. On the other hand, if to our initial evidence we add statements concerning the conductivity of pieces of other materials or concerning the number of older brothers of members of

---

emeroses are grue and hence the prediction that roses subsequently examined will be blue. The problem raised by such antecedents has been little noticed, but is no easier to meet than that raised by similarly perverse consequents.

other lecture audiences, this will not in the least affect the confirmation, according to our definition, of the hypothesis concerning copper or of that concerning this lecture audience. Since our definition is insensitive to the bearing upon hypotheses of evidence so related to them, even when the evidence is fully declared, the difficulty about accidental hypotheses cannot be explained away on the ground that such evidence is being surreptitiously taken into account.

A more promising suggestion is to explain the matter in terms of the effect of this other evidence not directly upon the hypothesis in question but *in*directly through other hypotheses that *are* confirmed, according to our definition, by such evidence. Our information about other materials does by our definition confirm such hypotheses as that all pieces of iron conduct electricity, that no pieces of rubber do, and so on; and these hypotheses, the explanation runs, impart to the hypothesis that all pieces of copper conduct electricity (and also to the hypothesis that none do) the character of lawlikeness—that is, amenability to confirmation by direct positive instances when found. On the other hand, our information about other lecture audiences *dis*confirms many hypotheses to the effect that all the men in one audience are third sons, or that none are; and this strips any character of lawlikeness from the hypothesis that all (or the hypothesis that none) of the men in *this* audience are third sons. But clearly if this course is to be followed, the circumstances under which hypotheses are thus related to one another will have to be precisely articulated.

The problem, then, is to define the relevant way in which such hypotheses must be alike. Evidence for the hypothesis that all iron conducts electricity enhances the lawlikeness of the hypothesis that all zirconium conducts electricity, but does not similarly affect the hypothesis that all the objects on my desk conduct electricity. Wherein lies the difference? The first two hypotheses fall under the broader hypothesis—call it "*H*"—that every class of things of the same material is uniform in conductivity; the first and third fall only under some such hypothesis as— call it "*K*"—that every class of things that are either all of the same material or all on a desk is uniform in conductivity. Clearly the important difference here is that evidence for a statement affirming that one of the classes covered by *H* has the property in question increases the credibility of any statement affirming that another such class has this property; while nothing of the sort holds true with respect to *K*. But this is only to say that *H* is lawlike and *K* is not. We are faced anew with the very problem we are trying to solve: the problem of distinguishing between lawlike and accidental hypotheses.

The most popular way of attacking the problem takes its cue from the fact that accidental hypotheses seem typically to involve some spatial or temporal restriction, or reference to some particular individual. They seem to concern the people in some particular room, or the objects on some particular person's desk; while lawlike hypotheses characteristically concern all ravens or all pieces of copper whatsoever. Complete generality is thus very often supposed to be a sufficient condition of lawlikeness; but to define this complete generality is by no means easy. Merely to require that the hypothesis contain no term naming, describing, or indicating a particular thing or location will obviously not be enough. The troublesome hypothesis that all emeralds are grue contains no such term; and where such a term does occur, as in hypotheses about men in *this room*, it can be suppressed in favor of some predicate (short or long, new or old) that contains no such term but applies only to exactly the same things. One might think, then, of excluding not only hypotheses that actually contain terms for specific individuals but also all hypotheses that are equivalent to others that do contain such terms. But, as we have just seen, to exclude only hypotheses of which *all* equivalents contain such terms is to exclude nothing. On the other hand, to exclude all hypotheses that have *some* equivalent containing such a term is to exclude everything; for even the hypothesis

All grass is green

has as an equivalent

All grass in London or elsewhere is green.

The next step, therefore, has been to consider ruling out predicates of certain kinds. A syntactically universal hypothesis is lawlike, the proposal runs, if its predicates are 'purely qualitative' or 'non-positional'.[11] This will obviously accomplish nothing if a purely qualitative

---

[11] Carnap took this course in his paper 'On the Application of Inductive Logic', *Philosophy and Phenomenological Research*, vol. 8 (1947), pp. 133–47, which is in part a reply to my 'A Query on Confirmation', cited in Note I.16. The discussion was continued in my note 'On Infirmities of Confirmation Theory', *Philosophy and Phenomenological Research*, vol. 8 (1947), pp. 149–51; and in Carnap's 'Reply to Nelson Goodman', same journal, same volume, pp. 461–2.

predicate is then conceived either as one that is equivalent to some expression free of terms for specific individuals, or as one that is equivalent to no expression that contains such a term; for this only raises again the difficulties just pointed out. The claim appears to be rather that at least in the case of a simple enough predicate we can readily determine by direct inspection of its meaning whether or not it is purely qualitative. But even aside from obscurities in the notion of 'the meaning' of a predicate, this claim seems to me wrong. I simply do not know how to tell whether a predicate is qualitative or positional, except perhaps by completely begging the question at issue and asking whether the predicate is 'well-behaved'—that is, whether simple syntactically universal hypotheses applying it are lawlike.

This statement will not go unprotested. "Consider", it will be argued, "the predicates 'blue' and 'green' and the predicate 'grue' introduced earlier, and also the predicate 'bleen' that applies to emeralds examined before time t just in case they are blue and to other emeralds just in case they are green. Surely it is clear", the argument runs, "that the first two are purely qualitative and the second two are not; for the meaning of each of the latter two plainly involves reference to a specific temporal position." To this I reply that indeed I do recognize the first two as well-behaved predicates admissible in lawlike hypotheses, and the second two as ill-behaved predicates. But the argument that the former but not the latter are purely qualitative seems to me quite unsound. True enough, if we start with "blue" and "green", then "grue" and "bleen" will be explained in terms of "blue" and "green" and a temporal term. But equally truly, if we start with "grue" and "bleen", then "blue" and "green" will be explained in terms of "grue" and "bleen" and a temporal term; "green", for example, applies to emeralds examined before time t just in case they are grue, and to other emeralds just in case they are bleen. Thus qualitativeness is an entirely relative matter and does not by itself establish any dichotomy of predicates. This relativity seems to be completely overlooked by those who contend that the qualitative character of a predicate is a criterion for its good behavior.

Of course, one may ask why we need worry about such unfamiliar predicates as "grue" or about accidental hypotheses in general, since we are unlikely to use them in making predictions. If our definition works for such hypotheses as are normally employed, isn't that all we need? In a sense, yes; but only in the sense that we need no definition, no theory of induction, and no philosophy of knowledge at all. We get along well enough without them in daily life and in scientific research. But if we seek a theory at all, we cannot excuse gross anomalies resulting from a proposed theory by pleading that we can avoid them in practice. The odd cases we have been considering are clinically pure cases that, though seldom encountered in practice, nevertheless display to best advantage the symptoms of a widespread and destructive malady.

We have so far neither any answer nor any promising clue to an answer to the question what distinguishes lawlike or confirmable hypotheses from accidental or nonconfirmable ones; and what may at first have seemed a minor technical difficulty has taken on the stature of a major obstacle to the development of a satisfactory theory of confirmation. It is this problem that I call the new riddle of induction.

5. The Pervasive Problem of Projection

At the beginning of this lecture, I expressed the opinion that the problem of induction is still unsolved, but that the difficulties that face us today are not the old ones; and I have tried to outline the changes that have taken place. The problem of justifying induction has been displaced by the problem of defining confirmation, and our work upon this has left us with the residual problem of distinguishing between confirmable and non-confirmable hypotheses. One might say roughly that the first question was "Why does a positive instance of a hypothesis give any grounds for predicting further instances?"; that the newer question was "What is a positive instance of a hypothesis?"; and that the crucial remaining question is "What hypotheses are confirmed by their positive instances?"

The vast amount of effort expended on the problem of induction in modern times has thus altered our afflictions but hardly relieved them. The original difficulty about induction arose from the recognition that anything may follow upon anything. Then, in attempting to define confirmation in terms of the converse of the consequence relation, we found ourselves with the distressingly similar difficulty that our definition would make any statement confirm any other. And now, after modifying our definition drastically, we still get the old devastating result that any statement will confirm any statement. Until we find a way of exercising some control over the hypotheses to be admitted, our definition makes no distinction whatsoever between valid and invalid inductive inferences.

The real inadequacy of Hume's account lay not in his descriptive approach but in the imprecision of his description. Regularities in experience, according to him, give rise to habits of expectation; and thus it is predictions conforming to past regularities that are normal or valid. But Hume overlooks the fact that some regularities do and some do not establish such habits; that predictions based on some regularities are valid while predictions based on other regularities are not. Every word you have heard me say has occurred prior to the final sentence of this lecture; but that does not, I hope, create any expectation that every word you will hear me say will be prior to that sentence. Again, consider our case of emeralds. All those examined before time t are green; and this leads us to expect, and confirms the prediction, that the next one will be green. But also, all those examined are grue; and this does not lead us to expect, and does not confirm the prediction, that the next one will be grue. Regularity in greenness confirms the prediction of further cases; regularity in grueness does not. To say that valid predictions are those based on past regularities, without being able to say *which* regularities, is thus quite pointless. Regularities are where you find them, and you can find them anywhere. As we have seen, Hume's failure to recognize and deal with this problem has been shared even by his most recent successors.

As a result, what we have in current confirmation theory is a definition that is adequate for certain cases that so far can be described only as those for which it is adequate. The theory works where it works. A hypothesis is confirmed by statements related to it in the prescribed way provided it is so confirmed. This is a good deal like having a theory that tells us that the area of a plane figure is one-half the base times the altitude, without telling us for what figures this holds. We must somehow find a way of distinguishing lawlike hypotheses, to which our definition of confirmation applies, from accidental hypotheses, to which it does not.

Today I have been speaking solely of the problem of induction, but what has been said applies equally to the more general problem of projection. As pointed out earlier, the problem of prediction from past to future cases is but a narrower version of the problem of projecting from any set of cases to others. We saw that a whole cluster of troublesome problems concerning dispositions and possibility can be reduced to this problem of projection. That is why the new riddle of induction, which is more broadly the problem of distinguishing between projectible and non-projectible hypotheses, is as important as it is exasperating.

Our failures teach us, I think, that lawlike or projectible hypotheses cannot be distinguished on any merely syntactical grounds or even on the ground that these hypotheses are somehow purely general in meaning. Our only hope lies in re-examining the problem once more and looking for some new approach. This will be my course in the final lecture.

IV

PROSPECTS FOR A
THEORY OF PROJECTION

1. A New Look at the Problem

The problem of confirmation, or of valid projection, is the problem of defining a certain relationship between evidence or base cases on the one hand, and hypotheses, predictions or projections on the other. Since numerous and varied attacks on the problem have brought us no solution, we may well ask ourselves whether we are still in any way misconceiving the nature of our task. I think the answer is affirmative: that we have come to mistake the statement of the required result for an unduly restricted statement of the means allowed for reaching that result.

What we want, indeed, is an accurate and general way of saying which hypotheses are confirmed by, or which projections are validly made from, any given evidence. Thus each particular case that arises does concern the relationship of given evidence to entertained hypotheses. But this does not imply that the only materials available to us in determining the relationship are the given evidence and the entertained hypotheses. In other words, while confirmation is indeed a relation between evidence and hypotheses, this does not mean that our definition of this relation must refer to nothing other than such evidence and hypotheses. The fact is that whenever we set about determining the validity of a given projection from a given base, we have and use a good deal of other relevant knowledge. I am not speaking of additional evidence statements, but rather of the record of past predictions actually made and their outcome. Whether these predictions—regardless of their success or failure—were valid or not remains in question; but that some were made and how they turned out is legitimately available information.

Proper use of such information will admittedly require some care. Surely we cannot subscribe to the naïve suggestion that induction is validated simply by its past successes. Every so often someone proclaims that the whole problem is solved just by recognizing that the prediction of future from past cases of a hypothesis is justified by the success of past predictions according to the hypothesis. Critics quickly point out that all the questions that arise about the validity of predicting future cases from past ones arise also about the validity of predicting future successes from past ones. But the fact that legitimately available information has been ineptly used should not lead us to discard it. In our present straits, we cannot afford to deprive ourselves of any honest means that may prove to be helpful.

I think we should recognize, therefore, that our task is to define the relation of confirmation or valid projection between evidence and hypothesis in terms of anything that does not beg the question, that meets our other demands for acceptable terms of explanation, and that may reasonably be supposed to be at hand when a question of inductive validity arises. This will include, among other things, some knowledge of past predictions and their successes and failures. I suppose that seldom, if ever, has there been any explicit proposal to preclude use of such knowledge in dealing with our problem. Rather, a long-standing habit of regarding such knowledge as irrelevant has led us to ignore it almost entirely. Thus what I am suggesting is less a reformulation of our problem than a reorientation: that we regard ourselves as coming to the problem not empty-headed but with some stock of knowledge, or of accepted statements, that may fairly be used in reaching a solution.

Nevertheless, this slight reorientation gives our problem quite a new look. For if we start with past projections as well as with evidence and hypotheses, our task becomes that of defining valid projection—or projectibility—on the basis of actual projections. Clearly this is a typical problem of dispositions. Given the manifest predicate "projected" and certain other information, we have to define the dispositional predicate "projectible." And this, as we have seen, resolves itself into the problem of projecting the predicate "projected". At first, this may be disheartening; for it looks as if we shall have to solve the problem of projection before we can deal with it—as if we must define valid projection before we can validly project "projected". But matters are not really that bad. Our ultimate aim is to define valid projection, or projectibility, in full generality. But this can also be regarded as a specific problem of projectibility: as the problem of projecting the specific predicate "projected", or in other words of defining the specific dispositional predicate "projectible". As I particularly remarked earlier,[1] there is no reason at

---

[1] See the remark in II.3 concerning a small note of comfort.

all why we cannot attempt to deal with a specific problem of dispositions before we have solved the general problem. And in the case of the specific problem of defining the predicate "projectible", the stakes are high; for if we succeed in solving it, we thereby solve the general problem. In effect, the general problem of dispositions has been reduced to the problem of projecting the specific predicate "projected".

The reorientation of our problem may be portrayed in somewhat more figurative language. Hume thought of the mind as being set in motion making predictions by, and in accordance with, regularities in what it observed. This left him with the problem of differentiating between the regularities that do and those that do not thus set the mind in motion. We, on the contrary, regard the mind as in motion from the start, striking out with spontaneous predictions in dozens of directions, and gradually rectifying and channeling its predictive processes. We ask not how predictions come to be made, but how—granting they are made—they come to be sorted out as valid and invalid. Literally, of course, we are not concerned with describing how the mind works but rather with describing or defining the distinction it makes between valid and invalid projections.

2. Actual Projections

A hypothesis will be said to be *actually projected* when it is adopted after some of its instances have been examined and determined to be true, and before the rest have been examined. The hypothesis need not be true, or lawlike, or even reasonable; for we are speaking here not of what ought to be projected but of what is in fact projected. Moreover, we are not concerned with the question whether a hypothesis is projected in the tenseless sense that there is some past, present or future time at which it is projected. We are concerned at any given time only with projections that have already been made.

Notice especially that even if all the instances examined up to a given time are favorable, and even if the hypothesis is true, still it may perhaps not be actually projected at that (or any other) time. Actual projection involves the overt, explicit formulation and adoption of the hypothesis —the actual prediction of the outcome of the examination of further cases. That the hypothesis could—or even could legitimately—have been projected at that time is at this stage beside the point. Just here lies the difference between starting from hypotheses and instances alone and starting from actual projections.

A full and exact explanation of actual projection would require much more careful statement of, for example, what is meant by adoption of a hypothesis. Obviously, affirmation as certainly true is not demanded, but rather something like affirmation as sufficiently more credible than alternative hypotheses. We could easily embroil ourselves in endless discussion of this and similar questions; but our purposes no more call for detailed answers to such questions than the development of ordinary confirmation theory calls for precise explanation of how evidence is acquired or of just what is involved in the acceptance of observation statements. There all we need do is indicate roughly what we mean by observation or evidence statements, and then proceed to the question of confirmation, assuming that some statements have been taken as evidence statements. The utility of determining that a hypothesis is confirmed by such statements will indeed depend upon their being genuinely accepted evidence statements; but our definition of the confirmation relation is largely independent of this consideration. Similarly, we need here only a summary sketch of what is meant by saying that a hypothesis is actually projected. We can then proceed to our definitional task, assuming that certain hypotheses are taken to have been projected at certain times. The utility of decisions based upon applications of our definition will, again, depend upon whether these projections have been made in fact; but definition of the relation between the projected and the projectible is, again, largely independent of this consideration.[2]

In what follows I shall make frequent use of certain convenient terms that call for brief explanation. Whether or not a hypothesis is actually projected at a given time, such instantiations of it as have already been determined to be true or false may be called respectively its *positive* and its *negative* instances or cases at that time. All the remaining instances are *undetermined* cases. For example, if the hypothesis is

All emeralds are green

and *e* is an emerald, then

Emerald *e* is green

---

[2] In other words, if we have determined that statements E, E', etc. stand to hypothesis H in the relationship specified by an adequate definition of confirmation, still the question whether H is a confirmed hypothesis will depend on whether E, E', etc. are actually evidence statements. Similarly, if we have determined that statements P, P', etc. stand to hypothesis K in the relationship specified by an adequate definition of projectibility, still the question whether K is a projectible hypothesis will depend on whether P, P', etc. are actually projected hypotheses. But see IV.4 below.

is a positive case when e has been found to be green, a negative case when e has been found not to be green, and an undetermined case when e has not yet been found either to be green or not to be green. The emeralds named in the positive cases constitute the *evidence class* for the hypothesis at the time in question, while the emeralds not named in any of the positive or negative cases constitute the *projective class* for the hypothesis at that time. A hypothesis for which there are some positive or some negative cases up to a given time is said to be *supported* or to be *violated* at that time. A violated hypothesis is false; but a false hypothesis may at a given time be unviolated. If a hypothesis has both positive and negative cases at a given time, it is then both supported and violated; while if it has no cases determined as yet, it is neither. A hypothesis without any remaining undetermined cases is said to be *exhausted*.

Now according to my terminology, adoption of a hypothesis constitutes actual projection only if at the time in question the hypothesis has some undetermined cases, some positive cases, and no negative cases. That is to say, I shall not speak of a hypothesis as being actually projected at any time when it is exhausted, unsupported, or violated. Obviously, adoption of an exhausted hypothesis involves nothing that we want to call projection. And convenience seems best served by denying the term "projection" to the adoption of a hypothesis without favorable direct evidence or in the face of direct counterevidence. Thus while a given hypothesis may undergo projection, violation, and exhaustion, the projection must antedate the violation and the exhaustion.

When all the undetermined cases of a hypothesis are future cases, its projection is a prediction. Very often, however, undetermined cases may be past cases; and here we have a projection that is not a prediction. Of course, the *determination* of an undetermined case is always later than the projection in question; but such a case may nevertheless be a statement of what has happened prior to that projection. To predict the outcome of the examination of a statement is not tantamount to predicting the (perhaps past) event described by that statement. Since pragmatism has sometimes fostered confusion concerning this point,[3] we should take particular care to remember, for example, that a hypothesis may remain unviolated at a given time even though some of its past-instance-statements are in fact false; for the violation of a hypothesis consists rather

---

[3] Some versions of pragmatism vacillate deftly between truism and patent falsehood, claiming the impregnability of the one and the importance of the other. It is urged that the truth and significance of a hypothesis lie in the accuracy of its predictions. Does this mean that all that counts is whether the hypothesis is true of the future? This is utterly absurd; for it makes the already violated statement "All emeralds are bleen" true if all emeralds not examined before *t* are green. Does the doctrine mean, then, that the only way of testing a hypothesis in the future is by tests in the future? This is absurdly true. Since a hypothesis is true only if true for all its cases, it is true only if true for all its future and all its undetermined cases; but equally, it is true only if true for all its past and all its determined cases. The pragmatist may perhaps be insisting rather that all we can learn even about past cases is by means of future experience; but this again is correct only if it amounts to saying, quite needlessly, that all we can learn in the future, even about past cases, is what we can learn in the future.

I am suggesting not that pragmatism is utterly wrong or empty but that it must be careful to distinguish its theses from wrong pronouncements to the effect that truth for future cases is sufficient for the truth of a hypothesis, and also from empty pronouncements to the effect that true hypotheses are true and that future tests are future.

in one of its instances having been *already* determined to be false.

What we have to work with at any given time, then, is a record of projections of a mass of heterogeneous hypotheses at various times. Some of these hypotheses have been violated since the time when they were projected. Others have successfully passed such further tests as they have undergone; but among these are some hypotheses that, since they have by now had all their instances examined and determined to be true, are exhausted and can no longer be projected. Some of the hypotheses projected are false. Some are bizarre. And some are at odds with others. Such is our raw material.

Obviously, not all the hypotheses that are projected are lawlike or legitimately projectible; and not all legitimately projectible hypotheses are actually projected. Hence we come to the task of defining projectibility—of projecting the predicate "projected" to the predicate "projectible". This problem is complex in more ways than one. It calls for elimination as well as expansion.[4] We face the twofold task of ruling out actually projected hypotheses that are not to be countenanced as projectible, and of bringing in legitimately projectible hypotheses that have not been actually projected—the twofold problem of projected unprojectibles and unprojected projectibles.

3. Resolution of Conflicts

We may concentrate at present upon simple universal hypotheses in categorical or hypothetical form—that is, upon hypotheses ascribing a certain predicate either to

---

[4] Cf. Note II.18.

everything in the universe of discourse or to everything to which a certain other predicate applies. Moreover, projectibility at a time must be our first concern; any question of defining temporally unqualified projectibility will have to wait.

The obvious first step in our weeding-out process is to eliminate all projected hypotheses that have since been violated. Such hypotheses, as already remarked, can no longer be projected, and are thus henceforth unprojectible. On similar grounds, all hypotheses having no remaining unexamined instances are likewise to be ruled out. However, neither the violated nor the exhausted hypotheses are thereby denied to have been projectible at an earlier time.

Not nearly so obvious are the further steps to be taken in order to eliminate projected hypotheses that, even though neither violated nor exhausted, are nevertheless unlawlike. Suppose, for example, that we are now at the time in question in the example of the preceding lecture, when all emeralds examined have been green; and suppose that the hypothesis that all emeralds are grue is projected. How are we to exclude it? We cannot simply assume that no such projection is ever actually made. Such illegitimate hypotheses are in fact adopted at times; and if I labored under any blissful delusion to the contrary, you could readily dispel it by arbitrarily adopting one.

Projections of this sort, however, will often *conflict* with other projections. If the hypothesis that all emeralds are green is also projected, then the two projections disagree for unexamined emeralds. In saying these projections thus conflict, we are indeed assuming that there is some unexamined emerald to which only one of the two consequent-predicates applies; but it is upon just this assumption that the problem arises at all. Yet how are we to devise a rule that will make the proper choice between these conflicting projections? We have noted that "green" and "grue" seem to be quite symmetrically related to each other. Are we any better off now than before to formulate the distinction between them?

The answer, I think, is that we must consult the record of past projections of the two predicates.[5] Plainly "green", as a veteran of earlier and many more projections than "grue", has the more impressive biography. The predicate "green", we may say, is much better *entrenched* than the predicate "grue".

We are able to draw this distinction only because we start from the record of past actual projections. We could not draw it starting merely from hypotheses and the evidence for them. For every time that "green" either was actually projected or—so to speak—could have been projected, "grue" also might have been projected; that is to say, whenever such a hypothesis as

All so-and-sos are green

was supported, unviolated, and unexhausted, the hypothesis

All so-and-sos are grue

was likewise supported, unviolated, and unexhausted.[6] Thus if we count all the occasions when each hypothesis

---

[5] A predicate "Q" is said to be projected when a hypothesis such as "All P's are Q's" is projected.

[6] The interpretation of "could have been projected" introduced here is further discussed below, in the first paragraph of Section 4. Suppose that all occurrences of "green" up to t and all later occurrences of "blue" are taken as 'tokens' of a single word. The

was in this sense available for projection, the two predicates have equal status. The significant difference appears only if we consider just those occasions when each predicate was actually projected.

After having declared this so emphatically, I must immediately modify it in one way. The entrenchment of a predicate results from the actual projection not merely of that predicate alone but also of all predicates coextensive with it. In a sense, not the word itself but the class it selects is what becomes entrenched, and to speak of the entrenchment of a predicate is to speak elliptically of the entrenchment of the extension of that predicate. On the other hand, the class becomes entrenched only through the projection of predicates selecting it; entrenchment derives from the use of language. But differences of tongue, use of coined abbreviations, and other variations in vocabulary do not prevent accrual of merited entrenchment.[7] Moreover, no entrenchment accrues from the

---

name of that word—i.e. the syntactic predicate applying to all and only these occurrences—will indeed be ill entrenched. But each occurrence of the word will fortify the entrenchment of each of the others if and only if all are coextensive. Briefly, the entrenchment of a word does not depend upon the entrenchment of its name. Hence while the problem of projectibility may arise at any syntactic level, my treatment is applicable at all levels and does not, as has sometimes been charged, merely push the problem up from each level to the one above.

[7] And all coextensive *replicas* of a predicate inscription or utterance (all coextensive 'tokens' of the same predicate 'type') will have equal entrenchment, determined by the total number of projections of all these replicas and all other utterances coextensive with them. On the other hand, the entrenchment of an utterance will not be increased by the projection of replicas of the utterance that are not coextensive with it.

repeated projection of a word except where the word has the same extension each time.

One principle for eliminating unprojectible projections, then, is that a projection is to be ruled out if it conflicts with the projection of a much better entrenched predicate. Conflicts may, of course, occur between projections of two predicates that are almost equally well or ill entrenched; but such conflicts are to be resolved in other ways and do not concern us here.[8] Our principle is inoperative where there is reasonable doubt about one predicate being more solidly entrenched than the other; it takes effect only where the difference is great enough to be obvious. Our primitive relation is that obtaining between any two predicates such that the first is much better entrenched than the second.

Like Hume, we are appealing here to past recurrences, but to recurrences in the explicit use of terms as well as to recurrent features of what is observed. Somewhat like Kant, we are saying that inductive validity depends not only upon what is presented but also upon how it is organized; but the organization we point to is effected by the use of language and is not attributed to anything inevitable

---

[8] Some conflicts between projections of equally well entrenched predicates may be resolved through conflict of one or both with projections of much better entrenched predicates; others will be resolved by means to be outlined in Section 5 below. But in many other cases the decision must await further evidence —a crucial experiment. Our task is not to resolve all conflicts between hypotheses, but only those where a question of legitimacy, or validity, is involved. To 'eliminate' a hypothesis as unprojectible obviously does not involve rejecting it as untrue; for while all consequences of a projectible hypothesis that is accepted as true must themselves be accepted as true, many of them (e.g. those that are unsupported or exhausted) will be unprojectible.

or immutable in the nature of human cognition. To speak very loosely, I might say that in answer to the question what distinguishes those recurrent features of experience that underlie valid projections from those that do not, I am suggesting that the former are those features for which we have adopted predicates that we have habitually projected.

My proposal by no means amounts to ruling unfamiliar predicates out of court. In the first place, entrenchment and familiarity are not the same. An entirely unfamiliar predicate may be very well entrenched, as we have seen, if predicates coextensive with it have often been projected; and another way a new predicate can acquire entrenchment will be explained presently. Again, a very familiar predicate may be rather poorly entrenched, since entrenchment depends upon frequency of projection rather than upon mere frequency of use. But in the second place, any wholesale elimination of unfamiliar predicates would result in an intolerable stultification of language. New and useful predicates like "conducts electricity" and "is radioactive" are always being introduced and must not be excluded simply because of their novelty. So far our rule legislates against such predicates only to the extent of eliminating projections of them that conflict with projections of much better entrenched predicates. Not predicates but certain projected hypotheses are being eliminated; and in each case the elimination is based upon specific comparison with an overriding hypothesis, not merely upon general grounds of the youth or oddity of the predicate projected. In framing further rules, we must continue to be on guard against throwing out all that is new along with all that is bad. Entrenched capital, in protecting itself, must yet allow full scope for free enterprise. (See IV.5.)

On several scores, then, our present approach is

altogether different from any mere dismissal of unfamiliar predicates. But an objection of a quite different sort might now be raised. Are we not trusting too blindly to a capricious Fate to see to it that just the right predicates get themselves comfortably entrenched? Must we not explain why, in cases of conflict like those illustrated, the really projectible predicate happens to have been the earlier and more often projected? And in fact wasn't it projected so often *because* its projection was so often obviously legitimate, so that our proposal begs the question? I think not. To begin with, what I am primarily suggesting is that the superior entrenchment of the predicate projected is in these cases a sufficient even if not necessary indication of projectibility; and I am not much concerned with whether the entrenchment or the projectibility comes first. But even if the question is taken as a genetic one, the objection seems to me ill-founded. In the case of new predicates, indeed, the legitimacy of any projection has to be decided on the basis of their relationship to older predicates; and whether the new ones will come to be frequently projected depends upon such decisions. But in the case of our main stock of well-worn predicates, I submit that the judgment of projectibility has derived from the habitual projection, rather than the habitual projection from the judgment of projectibility. The reason why only the right predicates happen so luckily to have become well entrenched is just that the well entrenched predicates have thereby become the right ones.

If our critic is asking, rather, why projections of predicates that have become entrenched happen to be those projections that will turn out to be *true*, the answer is that we do not by any means know that they will turn out to be true. When the time comes, the hypothesis that all emeralds are green may prove to be false, and the hypothesis that all are grue prove to be true. We have no guarantees. The criterion for the legitimacy of projections cannot be truth that is as yet undetermined. Failure to recognize this was responsible, as we saw, for some of the worst misconceptions of the problem of induction.

4. Presumptive Projectibility

The principle used above for resolving conflicts now needs to be developed into a more explicit and general rule. In what follows, I shall use "antecedent" and "consequent" for, respectively, the predicate of the antecedent and the predicate of the consequent of a conditional hypothesis. Two hypotheses are unequal in entrenchment if one has a better entrenched antecedent than the other and a no-less-well entrenched consequent, or has a better-entrenched consequent and a no-less-well entrenched antecedent. Two hypotheses conflict if neither follows from the other (and the fact that both are supported, unviolated, and unexhausted) and they ascribe to something two different predicates such that only one actually applies.

Our rudimentary principle may first be strengthened in an important way. How are we to deal with an undesirable hypothesis such as H_1

All emeralds are grue,

if it is projected when no legitimate conflicting hypothesis happens to be projected? We may still rule out H_1 on the ground that it conflicts with a non-projected hypothesis—e.g. K

All emeralds are green
—that has a no-less-well entrenched antecedent-predicate and a much better entrenched consequent-predicate, and is supported and unviolated. In effect, this is to say that H_1 conflicts with a hypothesis, containing suitably entrenched predicates, that was not projected but that could have been projected. "Could have been projected" is a non-toxic locution here, used only to say that at the time in question the hypothesis is supported, unviolated and unexhausted.[9] Now we particularly noted earlier that the entrenchment of a predicate has to be determined solely on the basis of *actual* projections; but once the entrenchment of the predicates concerned has been determined, we are free to make reference to hypotheses that, though actual,[10] are not actually projected but that merely, in the

---

[9] It must be borne in mind that a hypothesis can be projected only when it is unexhausted; hence when we assume for purposes of an illustration that a given hypothesis is or could be projected at a given time, we assume that it then has instances yet to be determined. In the case of K above, its being unexhausted follows from the requirement that it conflict with H_1. By the usage explained above, hypotheses actually projected at a given time are included among those that could have been projected at that time. That a hypothesis could have been projected does not, however, imply that it could legitimately have been projected.

[10] A hypothesis or other statement is actual, tenselessly speaking, if uttered or inscribed at any time—past, present, or future. A hypothesis may thus be actual without ever having been projected up to a given time. Indeed, there may well be actual hypotheses that could be projected at various times but are not projected at any time. Some, for example, may be uttered only after they have been violated or exhausted, or only before any of their instances have been examined, or only in the course of their denial.

precise sense just defined, could have been projected. Thus we no longer need to depend upon an appropriate hypothesis having actually been projected in order to eliminate an illegitimate conflicting one.

Let us now try framing a general rule and then consider how it applies to further cases. Since only supported, unviolated, and unexhausted hypotheses are projectible, we may confine our attention to these for the present. Among such hypotheses, H will be said to override H' if the two conflict and if H is the better entrenched and conflicts with no still better entrenched hypothesis.[11] Our rule reads: A hypothesis is *projectible* if all conflicting hypotheses are overridden, *unprojectible* if overridden, and *nonprojectible* if in conflict with another hypothesis and neither is overridden. Thus, for example, H_1 is overridden by K, and so is unprojectible, when all emeralds examined before t are found to be grue and hence green.[12]

----

[11]So stated, this covers only hierarchies of at most three supported, unviolated, unexhausted, and successively better entrenched and conflicting hypotheses. Since only marked differences in degree of entrenchment are taken into account, no hierarchy will have many members. But hierarchies of more than three members can be covered if necessary by making the definition more general so that a hypothesis is overridden if it is the bottom member of a hierarchy that has an even number of members, that is maximal in that it cannot be extended upward, and minimal in that each hypothesis conflicts only with adjacent ones.

[12] Specifications of the available evidence are often elliptical in this discussion. In the present case, for example, we tacitly assume also that some emeralds have been examined before t, while some things other than emeralds may or may not have been found to be green or of some other color.

Suppose, however, the predicate "grund" applies to all things examined up to a certain time t that are green and to all things not so examined that are round; and suppose that at some time not later than t, when all emeralds examined have been found to be green, H_2

All emeralds are grund

is projected. How are we to deal with this unwelcome hypothesis in the absence of conflict with K? Of course, if all examined emeralds have also been found to be square, then H_2 will be overridden by H_3

All emeralds are square.

But if all emeralds examined before t have been found to be green but either none has been examined for shape or some have been found to be square and others not square, then H_3 is either unsupported or violated and so cannot override H_2. Here, however, H_2 conflicts with the equally well entrenched hypothesis H_4

All emeralds are grare,

(where a thing is grare if either green and examined before t, or not so examined and square) so that both H_2 and H_4 are nonprojectible.[13] That is, they are not projecti-

---

[13] When some emeralds have been found to be square and others round, we can retreat from these two hypotheses to the weaker hypothesis "All emeralds are square or round", which does not conflict with them but is projectible whereas they are not. If statistical hypotheses are taken into account, H_2 may be *un*projectible, being overridden by some hypothesis concerning shape distribution among emeralds; but the treatment of statistical hypotheses is a complicated matter requiring redefinition of support, violation, conflict, and so on.

ble or unprojectible at the time in question. They can neither be welcomed as projectible nor dismissed as unprojectible; and thus, with the evidence as stated, the choice of H_1 over both H_2 and H_4 is validated. But nonprojectibility does not in general imply illegitimacy. Even the best entrenched conflicting hypotheses are nonprojectible when further evidence is needed to decide between them.[14]

Suppose, though, all emeralds examined before t have been both green and round. Under these circumstances, since H_3 is violated and such hypotheses as H_4 are overridden by H_5

All emeralds are round,

H_2 escapes competent conflict and qualifies as projectible. And plainly, projection of H_2 is harmless where the evidence thus makes projectible two well entrenched hypotheses, H_5 and K

All emeralds are green,

such that H_2 follows from their conjunction. This is *not* to say that consequences of projectible hypotheses are always projectible; for some such consequences are unsupported or exhausted. But a consequence of a projectible hypothesis meets two of the requirements for projectibility: it is unviolated, and all conflicting hypotheses are overridden. And thus H_2, since also supported and unexhausted by the evidence given, is projectible.

Still, are we content to say that H_2 is projectible in this case? Lingering reluctance to do so arises, it seems, from

---

[14] Differences in *degree* of projectibility among nonprojectible, and other, hypotheses will be considered in the following section.

confusing two senses of "projectible". In one sense, a hypothesis is projectible if support normally makes it credible. In another sense, a hypothesis is projectible only when the actual evidence supports and makes it credible.[15] In the first sense, K is projectible. In the second sense, intended throughout most of what follows, K is not projectible when deprived, by evidence that violates or exhausts it or leaves it in conflict with hypotheses that are not overridden, of its normal capacity to derive credibility from support. On the other hand H_2, though normally not projectible, may be relieved, by evidence that neither violates nor exhausts it but overrides all conflicting hypotheses, of its normal incapacity to derive credibility from support. In sum, just as a normally projectible hypothesis may lose projectibility under unfavorable evidence, so a hypothesis not normally projectible may gain projectibility under sufficiently favorable evidence.

Besides hypotheses having troublesome consequents, we must also deal with those having troublesome antecedents.[16] Let the predicate "emeruby" apply to emeralds examined for color before t and to rubies not examined before t; and as before, let us suppose that all emeralds

---

[15] In a third sense, a hypothesis is projectible only if projectible in both these senses. Robert Schwartz is planning a paper on some of the several varieties of projectibility.

[16] Earlier, considering consequents alone, I have spoken of the entrenchment of a predicate as depending on past projections of the predicate—i.e. upon occurrences as consequent of projected hypotheses. The entrenchment of an antecedent similarly depends upon its occurrences as antecedent of projected hypotheses. The entrenchment of a given predicate as antecedent and as consequent may not always be equal; but in saying that the consequent of one hypothesis is, for example, much better entrenched than

examined for color prior to time t are green. Thus at a time not later than t, all emerubies examined for color have been green. Yet clearly at this time a projection of H_6

All emerubies are green

is quite as invalid as is a projection of H_1 or H_2. Of course, if at the time in question some rubies have been examined for color and all so examined found to be red, then H_6 is overridden by the conflicting hypothesis H_7

All rubies are red.

But what if no rubies have been examined for color? If, say, all sapphires examined have been blue, H_6 will be non-projectible as the result of conflict with the no-less-well entrenched hypothesis

All sapphirubies are blue.

And indeed if we have found anything, say the Eiffel tower, of some color other than green, say black, H_6 will conflict with some such hypothesis as

All Eifferubies are black.

Suppose, though, that our evidence is confined to just the examined green emeralds—that, in effect, nothing else whatever has been examined for color. In this case, since even the sweeping hypothesis

All things are green

---

the consequent of another, I am always speaking of the comparative entrenchment of the two predicates *as consequents*. And likewise, in the case of antecedents, what is relevant is their entrenchment *as antecedents*.

will be projectible, its consequences—such as H_6—will be harmless.

Finally, as Donald Davidson has noted,[17] some hypotheses are misbegotten with respect to both antecedent and consequent. Consider H_8

All emerubies are gred.

If the evidence consists solely of green emeralds examined before t, this hypothesis is overridden by H_6. However, if evidence consisting solely of red rubies examined before t is added, then H_8 becomes projectible; for the formerly overriding hypothesis H_6 is now itself overridden by H_7. Furthermore, in this case H_8 follows from the two projectible hypotheses K and H_7.

No new consideration is required to show that

All emerubies are grund,

while not projectible if before t either no emeralds or rubies have been examined for shape or else some emeralds or rubies have been found not to be round, is projectible if all examined emeralds are green and all examined rubies round.

The effectiveness of our rule is increased when we take into account an aspect of entrenchment that we have so far ignored for the sake of simplicity. Let us, first, say that a predicate "P" is a parent of a given predicate "Q" if among the classes that "P" applies to is the extension of "Q";[18] for example, the predicate "army division" is a

---

[17] In "Emeroses by Other Names", *Journal of Philosophy*, vol. 63 (1966), pp. 778–80.

[18] A predicate, unlike a person, may have any number of parents. Note also that a parent predicate of "Q" is a parent of every predicate coextensive with "Q".

parent of the predicate "soldier in the 26th division". Now a novel predicate may inherit entrenchment from a parent predicate. Compare, for instance, the predicate "marble in bag B", applying to marbles in a bag just found, with the predicate "marble in zig A", applying to marbles in some quite helter-skelter selection. Suppose that each predicate is occurring for the first time as the antecedent of a projected hypothesis. Their direct or earned entrenchment is negligible and equal, but the former is the more comfortably settled by inheritance. Its parent predicate "bagful of marbles" has occurred as antecedent of many more projections than has any comparable parent of the predicate "marble in zig A". The inherited entrenchment of two predicates of about equal earned entrenchment is gauged by comparing the better entrenched among the parents of each. This could often call for difficult and delicate judgments except that we are concerned here as earlier only with differences gross enough to be easily discerned. It must be particularly noted, furthermore, that comparison of the inherited entrenchment of two predicates is in point only if neither has much greater earned entrenchment than the other. Earned entrenchment, so to speak, establishes the major levels of entrenchment, and only within these does inherited entrenchment effect a subsidiary grading. Thus a predicate is much better entrenched than another if the former either has much greater earned entrenchment than the latter or has about equal earned and much greater inherited entrenchment.

Our rule is now quite powerful, yielding the proper decision in a wide variety of cases while allowing for introduction of acceptable new predicates. Furthermore, although we began with actual projections, the rule obviously covers all hypotheses, whether projected or not; that is, a hypothesis not actually projected may be projectible according to the rule and may override other hypotheses. In effect, our rule offers us the following definitions: a hypothesis is *projectible* when and only when it is supported, unviolated, and unexhausted, and all such hypotheses that conflict with it are overridden; *nonprojectible* when and only when it and a conflicting hypothesis are supported, unviolated, unexhausted, and not overridden; and *unprojectible* when and only when it is unsupported, violated, exhausted, or overridden.

These formulae, though, are only provisional, and the projectibility here defined is at best *presumptive projectibility*. The sorting into three categories is gross and tentative. Hypotheses assigned to the same category may differ greatly in *degree* of projectibility; and the degree of projectibility of a given hypothesis may be affected by indirect evidence.

5. Comparative Projectibility

Among presumptively projectible hypotheses, the initial index of degree of projectibility is determined solely on the basis of comparative entrenchment. But what now demand special attention are the factors that result in a higher or lower ultimate index.

Consider, for example, the hypothesis H_9

All the marbles in bag B are red,

where B is one in a recently discovered stack S of bags of marbles; and let us suppose that the evidence is such that H_9 is presumptively projectible. With a well entrenched consequent but with an antecedent having no earned and only moderate inherited entrenchment, H_9 will not have a high initial projectibility index. Now suppose further that we have emptied a few other bags from the stack and have found that while the marbles in different bagfuls so examined sometimes differ in color, still all the marbles in each bagful are of the same color. This information, which of course furnishes no direct evidence for or against H_9, appreciably enhances the projectibility of H_9 in the following way: Each time we find that all the marbles in a given bagful are of the same color, we establish a positive instance of the hypothesis G

Every bagful in stack S is uniform in color;[19]

by thus confirming G we increase the credibility of its undetermined instances, among them the statement G_1

Bagful B is uniform in color;

and by so increasing the credibility of G_1, we increase the credibility H_9 derives from its own positive cases. In short, the evidence for G, by increasing the credibility of G_1, increases the projectibility of H_9.

---

[19] I have supposed that every marble from each of the emptied bags has been examined for color; but all that is really required is that from each bag we have examined enough to be willing to accept, as a positive case for G, the statement that all the marbles in that bagful are of a certain color. As pointed out earlier, the nature of the examination that yields a determined case of a hypothesis is irrelevant to our central problem. Just as a glance at one side of a marble may be enough for acceptance of the evidence statement that the marble is red, so a glance at a bagful may be enough for acceptance of the evidence statement that all the marbles in it are, say, green. Projected hypotheses, in other words, may sometimes be accepted as positive cases for other hypotheses.

This is not to say that the evidence for G in any way favors H_9 as against such a hypothesis as

All the marbles in bag B are blue.

Obviously G is entirely neutral as between hypotheses that differ only in what single color they ascribe to all the marbles in B. But if one among these hypotheses is presumptively projectible[20]—as we have here assumed H_9 to be—then the credibility transmitted from positive to undetermined cases of this hypothesis increases as the evidence for G increases. A hypothesis cannot be confirmed without positive cases, but its positive cases confirm it only to the extent that it is projectible. The number of positive cases for a hypothesis and its degree of projectibility are quite distinct factors in its confirmation.

Clearly, the projectibility of H_9 may be affected by other information through other hypotheses related to H_9 much as G is. Let us say that G is a *positive overhypothesis of H_9*, and in general that a hypothesis is a positive overhypothesis of a second, if the antecedent and consequent of the first are parent predicates of, respectively, the antecedent and consequent of the second. Thus if B is a small bag and in Utah, the hypotheses

All small bagfuls of marbles are uniform in color,

All bagfuls of marbles in Utah are uniform in color,

---

[20] Not more than one such hypothesis is presumptively projectible. For a presumptively projectible hypothesis must be supported; and if a hypothesis ascribing one color to all the marbles in B is supported, then any hypothesis ascribing a different color to them is violated.

All bagfuls of marbles in stack S are uniformly of some warm color,

and others will be positive overhypotheses of H_9; and H_9 as presumptively projectible and thus supported and unviolated, follows from each of them. But a hypothesis—whether overhypothesis or not—does not automatically transmit its own degree of projectibility to a consequence. How much the projectibility of H_9 is reinforced by such overhypotheses as these will depend upon several factors.

In some cases, the projectibility of a hypothesis will not be increased at all even by a positive overhypothesis that is well supported and unviolated. An overhypothesis that is not presumptively projectible has no reinforcing effect, for such a hypothesis can be used to tie totally irrelevant information to a given hypothesis. If, for example, many naval fleets have been examined and each found to be uniform in color, and if the predicate "bagleet" applies just to naval fleets and to bagful B of marbles, then

Every bagleet is uniform in color

is an unviolated, well supported, positive overhypothesis of H_9. Yet obviously our information concerning naval fleets contributes nothing to the projectibility of H_9. Only presumptively projectible overhypotheses count; and the one concerning bagleets is not presumptively projectible; it will conflict with such a hypothesis as

All bagmarks are mixed in color

where "bagmark" applies just to makes of cars and to bagful B.

Moreover the effect that an overhypothesis has will depend upon its degree of projectibility. A highly projectible overhypothesis supported by even a few positive cases may considerably enhance the projectibility of a given hypothesis. On the other hand, an overhypothesis of negligible projectibility, no matter how well supported, will have little more influence than one that is not even presumptively projectible. Thus the impact that our information concerning other bagfuls in stack S has upon the projectibility of H_9 will depend upon the projectibility of G. And the projectibility of G will of course be its initial projectibility index as modified by overhypotheses of G. Hence determination of the degree of projectibility of H_9 will require determination of the projectibility of such overhypotheses as G; and this will in turn require determination of the projectibility of such overhypotheses of G as J

Every stack of marbles in Utah is homogeneous in color variegation,

(where a stack is homogeneous in color variegation just in case either every bagful in it is uniform in color or else every bagful in it is mixed in color). But we need not fear that we have started upon an endless or even a very long journey; indeed, the end is already in sight. For since, quite plainly, no parent predicate of the consequent of J has any appreciable entrenchment, either direct or inherited, no overhypothesis of J will have more than an extremely low initial projectibility index. And as we shall see in a moment, when the initial index is negligible, the final degree of projectibility will also be negligible. Thus no overhypothesis of J will have any appreciable degree of projectibility, and so none can appreciably modify the initial projectibility of J. The projectibility of J, needed in determining the projectibility of G and so of H_9, is therefore determined without going to higher and higher levels.

Ordinarily, as we have seen, a hypothesis with one or both predicates negligibly entrenched will not be presumptively projectible. Unless it is a consequence of a better entrenched projectible hypothesis, a no-less-well entrenched conflicting hypothesis can usually be contrived. Furthermore, we can easily show that a hypothesis with a negligible initial projectibility index will have a negligible final degree of projectibility. A hypothesis gets a negligible index through having a predicate with virtually no earned or inherited entrenchment. Where zig A is, as before, some quite helter-skelter selection of marbles, the hypothesis

Everything in zig A is red

has a negligible initial projectibility index because the antecedent is without appreciable entrenchment. But now this antecedent, "in zig A", since it has no appreciable inherited entrenchment, can have no parent predicate with any appreciable entrenchment. And since any positive overhypothesis of our hypothesis must contain a parent predicate of "in zig A", every such overhypothesis will have only a negligible initial projectibility index. By similar argument every overhypothesis of such overhypotheses, and every hypothesis farther up in this hierarchy, will have a negligible initial index. But a hypothesis without an appreciable initial index can acquire increased projectibility only through an appreciably projectible overhypothesis. Thus in the hierarchy in question, a hypothesis at any level can acquire appreciable projectibility only through some overhypothesis at the next higher level; and the over-hypotheses at this next higher level are in the same predicament. Nowhere in this hierarchy do we reach a hypothesis that is appreciably projectible in its own right and thus capable of increasing the projectibility of hypotheses beneath it. Hence the initial negligible index of our hypothesis concerning zig A will remain unmodified; and any hypothesis with an extremely low initial index will have an extremely low final degree of projectibility.

This has two useful consequences. One, as we have already seen, is that the process of appraising the projectibility of a hypothesis need not run up through an endless hierarchy of overhypotheses. The other is that even when a hypothesis such as the one about zig A is presumptively projectible, its lack of any appreciable degree of projectibility can be inferred from its very low initial index.

Emphatic warnings must be issued at this point against some misunderstandings. In the first place, nothing I have said implies that a hypothesis with *more* than a negligible initial index may not have a considerably higher final degree of projectibility. For example, since a predicate with no earned entrenchment and a modest inheritance may have parent predicates of very appreciable entrenchment, a hypothesis containing this predicate may have overhypotheses with considerable power to increase projectibility. Moreover, even a hypothesis with a negligible initial index at one time may gain greatly in projectibility when circumstances change—for example, when the predicates in question become well-entrenched through frequent projection, or when new evidence violates conflicting hypotheses. All this, together with the already noted fact that some new predicates derive entrenchment from coextensive or from parent predicates, shows how groundless is the complaint that our theory excludes hypotheses with unfamiliar predicates.

The projectibility of and evidence for an overhypothesis are not the only factors that must be considered. Much depends also upon, so to speak, how closely the evidence for an overhypothesis is allied to the hypothesis in question, or in other words, upon how specific the overhypothesis is.[21] Information concerning bagfuls examined from stack S clearly has more bearing upon H_9 than upon a similar hypothesis concerning marbles in some bag in another stack in Utah—for example, the hypothesis H_{10}

All the marbles in bag W are red,

where W is a bag in stack T. Our examination of bagfuls from S provides us with exactly the same number of positive cases for the overhypothesis U

Every bagful of marbles in Utah is uniform in color

as it does for G

Every bagful of marbles in stack S is uniform in color.

Yet the information we have is plainly less effective in raising the projectibility of H_{10} through U than in raising the projectibility of H_9 through G. Briefly, where both projectibility and amount of support are equal, the effect

---

[21] Where the several hypotheses falling under an overhypothesis have antecedent-predicates that are not mutually exclusive, a further factor that must be taken into account is the extent of duplication in the evidence claimed by two or more of these hypotheses.

of overhypotheses varies inversely with their generality. Offhand it might seem that on the contrary the broader and more sweeping overhypotheses must have the greater effect. But this happens only where a more general hypothesis brings to bear a great deal more information—for example, where U is supported by the results of examining not only bagfuls from S but also many other bagfuls, perhaps including some from T. Where two equally projectible overhypotheses bring equal evidence to bear, the more specific one has the more powerful effect.

Thus the comparative effectiveness of different presumptively and appreciably projectible overhypotheses depends upon three factors. Where such hypotheses are equally specific and have equal supporting evidence, their effectiveness varies with their degree of projectibility. Where specificity and also degree of projectibility are equal, effectiveness varies with amount of support. And where degree of projectibility and also amount of support are equal, effectiveness varies with specificity.

Further elaboration of such details would be out of place here; for many of them are neither novel nor peculiar to my approach. It is no news that the projectibility of hypotheses is affected by certain related hypotheses, or that the effect of correlative information is the greater the more of it there is and the more closely it is allied to the hypothesis in question. And the suggestion has been made before that the explanation of differences in lawlikeness among hypotheses requires reference to certain 'background hypotheses'. But what has been commonly overlooked is the cardinal fact that the background hypotheses themselves depend for their effectiveness upon their projectibility; and I have therefore emphasized this aspect of the matter here.

So long as the treatment of comparative projectibility is confined within the realm of presumptively projectible hypotheses, a choice between conflicting hypotheses will never rest upon a difference in degree of projectibility, for no two presumptively projectible hypotheses conflict. On the other hand, a hypothesis is nonprojectible only if it conflicts with another that is about equally well-entrenched; and some such conflicts may be resolved if our treatment of comparative projectibility is extended to presumptively nonprojectible hypotheses. Although the initial indices of conflicting nonprojectible hypotheses will be about equal, the degrees of projectibility may differ enough to decide the issue. In other words, although neither of the hypotheses overrides the other, one may *outweigh* the other; and presumptively nonprojectible hypotheses that thus win over their competitors become projectible. The question then arises how such a hypothesis compares in overall projectibility with a presumptively projectible hypothesis having a lower degree of projectibility; but again, since such a pair of hypotheses never conflict, a unified measure of overall projectibility,[22] however valuable it may be, is not required for the resolution of any conflict.

In some cases, of course, the degrees of projectibility as well as the initial indices of conflicting presumptively projectible hypotheses may be equal, and further evidence —a 'crucial experiment'—is wanted. Sometimes such conflicting hypotheses, though presumptively nonprojectible, may be very well entrenched. Since positive overhypothe-

---

[22] By "degree of projectibility" I shall continue to refer to the degree calculated in the way outlined above rather than to the overall measure of projectibility mentioned but not defined here.

ses may raise but cannot lower the degree of projectibility of a hypothesis, we might suppose that a hypothesis with a high initial index must have a high degree of projectibility. But what we have not yet taken into account is that the projectibility of a hypothesis may often be decreased rather than increased by correlative information. If every examined bagful of marbles from stack S is mixed rather than uniform in color, then clearly the projectibility of H_9

All the marbles in bag B are red

will be thereby decreased. The evidence for M,

Every bagful in S is mixed in color,

reduces the credibility transmitted from the positive to the undetermined cases of H_9. Now while the antecedent of M is a parent predicate of the antecedent of H_9, the consequent of M is not a parent predicate of the consequent of H_9. Instead, the consequent of M is *complementary* to a parent predicate of the consequent of H_9 in that "mixed in color" applies to all and only those bagfuls in S to which "uniform in color" does not apply. Thus M, though syntactically positive, may be called a negative overhypothesis of H_9. The criteria of effectiveness are the same for a negative as for a positive overhypothesis; and the projectibility of a hypothesis is weakened through effective negative overhypotheses just as it is strengthened through effective positive ones. Accordingly, even when competing nonprojectible hypotheses are highly and equally entrenched, the adverse effects of negative overhypotheses upon them may differ greatly and the resultant degrees of projectibility be so unequal that one hypothesis clearly outweighs the other.

Under no circumstances, of course, could M and the positive overhypothesis G both qualify at once as effective overhypotheses; for if either is supported, the other is violated. Yet obviously if some bagfuls in S are uniform in color and others mixed, the projectibility of H_9 may be strengthened or weakened according as cases of the one kind or the other predominate. The effect of this mingled evidence will be exerted through a statistical overhypothesis affirming that most, or a certain percentage, of the bagfuls in S are uniform (or are mixed) in color. Here as before the effectiveness of such an overhypothesis will depend on its projectibility. Thus what has been said so far concerning the projectibility of simple universal hypotheses must eventually be extended to cover statistical hypotheses as well. But while the general way of doing this is clear enough, the details are too complicated for treatment here. Accordingly I shall carry on the convenient expository fiction that only universal hypotheses need enter into consideration.

Incidentally, when we were dealing exclusively with presumptively projectible hypotheses, negative overhypotheses did not enter into consideration; for since a hypothesis and any of its negative overhypotheses conflict, both cannot be presumptively projectible. Either the two are unequal in entrenchment in that one overrides the other and makes it unprojectible, or both are equal in entrenchment so that both are presumptively nonprojectible. Only in the latter case, and when our treatment of comparative projectibility takes in presumptively nonprojectible hypotheses, do negative overhypotheses as such call for explicit recognition.

One may contemplate the utility and consequences of

extending the treatment of comparative projectibility even further: to hypotheses that, though supported and unviolated and unexhausted, are unprojectible through being overridden. But I shall not pursue this here. Complications have already multiplied almost beyond manageability, with the degree of projectibility of a hypothesis being affected by numerous positive and negative over-hypotheses varying in projectibility, specificity, and supporting evidence.

To appraise the projectibility of a hypothesis, methodically taking all these factors into account, could be a discouraging task; but in practice we seldom need to go through all that. When faced with a conflict between two actually entertained hypotheses, we usually know quite well where to look for circumstances likely to make for a significant difference in projectibility. Moreover, the present inquiry has not been devoted to describing or prescribing a procedure. The concern here has been with definition rather than description, with theory rather than practice. The results are indeed intricate, incomplete, and often tentative, falling far short of a full and final theory. All I have offered is a study of some of the resources that a new approach offers us for dealing with a difficult problem. If you were expecting more, may I remind you of the title of this lecture?

6. Survey and Speculations

If I am at all correct, then, the roots of inductive validity are to be found in our use of language. A valid prediction is, admittedly, one that is in agreement with past regularities in what has been observed; but the difficulty has always been to say what constitutes such agreement.

The suggestion I have been developing here is that such agreement with regularities in what has been observed is a function of our linguistic practices. Thus the line between valid and invalid predictions (or inductions or projections) is drawn upon the basis of how the world is and has been described and anticipated in words.

You will remember that in our inspection of several interrelated problems we found that some of them could in effect be reduced to the problem of projectibility. Thus insofar as we have found a way of dealing with that problem, we have not only found a way of handling a neglected dimension of confirmation theory and so of answering the persistent residual question concerning induction, but we have also found a way of dealing with the problem of dispositions and the problem of possible entities.

A theory of projectibility or lawlikeness also removes one of the obstacles to a satisfactory treatment of counterfactual conditionals; but the problem of counterfactuals, as we saw, offers other difficulties of its own. One further suggestion, however, may perhaps help some here. I said earlier that the falsity of such a counterfactual[23] as V

If that penny (also) had been put in my pocket on VE day, it (also) would have been silver on VE day

results from the fact that the requisite general principle P

All the coins put in my pocket on VE day were silver on VE day,

even though true, is not lawlike. But this analysis is incomplete. For suppose that circumstances are such as to make

---

[23] The example used earlier (I.8) has here been altered a little to remove some ambiguities.

P lawlike; suppose, for example, that we have examined the sets of coins put into the pockets of many a different person on many a different day and have found that in each set all the coins are made of the same material, and suppose that much other reinforcing evidence is available. Still P, though thus rendered lawlike, will not sustain V which remains false. Even a true law is sometimes incapable of sustaining a counterfactual. The explanation, I think, is that the conflicting semifactual

If that penny (also) had been put in my pocket on VE day, it would have remained copper on VE day

is here at the same time upheld by the much stronger law

Coins remain of the same material regardless of mere changes in place.

The counterfactual V is invalidated not by lack of a law upholding it but by conflict with a more strongly upheld conditional. Thus adequate interpretation of a counterfactual seems to require attention to its conflicts with other conditionals, and to principles for resolving these conflicts. Along these lines, indeed, we may well be able to account for the falsity of such a counterfactual as

If that match had been scratched, it would not have been dry,

and so to answer even the most stubborn remaining question concerning counterfactual conditionals.

Our treatment of projectibility holds some promise in other directions. It may give us a way of distinguishing 'genuine' from merely 'artificial' kinds, or more genuine from less genuine kinds, and thus enable us to interpret ordinary statements affirming that certain things are or are not of the same kind, or are more akin than certain other things. For surely the entrenchment of classes is some measure of their genuineness as kinds; roughly speaking, two things are the more akin according as there is a more specific and better entrenched predicate that applies to both. An adequate theory of kinds should in turn throw light on some troublesome questions concerning the simplicity of ideas, laws, and theories. And it may also hint an approach to the problem of randomness; for in one important sense, at least, the examined cases of a hypothesis are the less random as they are the more akin—that is, roughly, as there is a more specific and better entrenched predicate that applies to them all. Let me illustrate in terms of two different sets of evidence for the hypothesis that every bagful of marbles in stack S is uniform in color: first, a set of examined bagfuls, all of them from the top layer of S; second, a set drawn from various layers, from the inside and outside of the stack, and so on. The predicate "on the top layer of S", which applies to every bagful in the first and less random set, has more (inherited) entrenchment than any equally narrow or specific predicate applying to everything in the second and more random set.

But none of these speculations should be taken for a solution. I am not offering any easy and automatic device for disposing of all, or indeed of any, of these problems. Ample warning of the distance from promising idea to tenable theory has been given by the complexities we have had to work through in developing our proposal concerning projectibility; and even this task is not complete in all details. I cannot reward your kind attention with the comforting assurance that all has been done, or with the perhaps almost as comforting assurance that nothing can be done. I have simply explored a not altogether familiar way of attacking some all too familiar problems.

INDEX